HEALTH AND SAFETY MANAGEMENT FOR TOUR AND PRODUCTION MANAGERS

and

SELF EMPLOYMENT IN THE LIVE MUSIC AND EVENTS INDUSTRY

A GUIDE FOR THE SELF EMPLOYED AND THOSE WHO USE THE SERVICES OF THE SELF EMPLOYED

Chris Hannam

ENTERTAINMENT TECHNOLOGY PRESS

Safety Series

Masquerade Club. Atlanta, Georgia. Photo: Kim Ray

HEALTH AND SAFETY MANAGEMENT FOR TOUR AND PRODUCTION MANAGERS

and

SELF-EMPLOYMENT IN THE LIVE MUSIC AND EVENTS INDUSTRY

A GUIDE FOR THE SELF-EMPLOYED AND THOSE WHO USE THE SERVICES OF THE SELF-EMPLOYED

Chris Hannam

Entertainment Technology Press

Health and Safety Management for Tour and Production Managers

and

Self-Employment in the Live Music and Events Industry

A Guide for the Self-Employed and those who use the services of the Self-Employed

© Chris Hannam

First published August 2015
Entertainment Technology Press Ltd
The Studio, High Green, Great Shelford, Cambridge CB22 5EG
Internet: www.etnow.com

ISBN 978 1 904031 86 4

A title within the
Entertainment Technology Press Safety Series
Series editor: John Offord

All rights reserved. No part of this publication may be reproduced in any material form (including photocopying or storing in any medium by electronic means and whether or not transiently or incidentally to some other use of this publication) without the written permission of the copyright holder except in accordance with the provisions of the Copyright, Designs and Patents Act 1988. Applications for the copyright holder's written permission to reproduce any part of this publication should be addressed to the publishers.
The contents of this publication are provided in good faith and neither The Author nor The Publisher can be held responsible for any errors or omissions contained herein. Any person relying upon the information must independently satisfy himself or herself as to the safety or any other implications of acting upon such information and no liability shall be accepted either by The Author or The Publisher in the event of reliance upon such information nor for any damage or injury arising from any interpretation of its contents. This publication may not be used in any process of risk assessment.

CODE / CH3-001_08-15

CONTENTS

ACKNOWLEDGEMENTS ... 11

HEALTH AND SAFETY MANAGEMENT FOR TOUR AND PRODUCTION MANAGERS ... 13
INTRODUCTION ... 15
Accident Costs ... 16
Iceberg of Workplace Injury Costs ... 18
Other key points to consider ... 18

THE HEALTH AND SAFETY AT WORK, ETC ACT 1974 ... 20
HEALTH AND SAFETY ENFORCEMENT ... 21
Powers of the enforcement authorities ... 21

LEGAL DUTIES UNDER THE HEALTH AND SAFTY AT WORK ACT ... 23
Duties of Employers ... 23
Duties of Employees ... 23
Duties of the Self-Employed ... 24

THE HEALTH AND SAFTY POLICY ... 25
CULTURE ... 26
THE MANAGEMENT OF HEALTH AND SAFETY AT WORK REGULATIONS ... 28
PLAN ... 30
DO ... 30
CHECK ... 31
ACT ... 31

SAFE SYSTEMS OF WORK (SSoW) ... 31
Hazard and Risk ... 31
Legislation ... 31
Components of a Safe System ... 31
When is a SSoW required? ... 31

METHOD STATEMENTS, PERMITS TO WORK AND RISK ASSESSMENTS.........33
Method Statements.........33
Permits to Work.........33
Risk Assessments.........34
What's the likelihood of an accident?.........38
What could be the worst possible outcome of an accident?.........38
Risk Class.........39
Information.........39
Current Controls ***.........40
Do your current controls meet the standards set by legal requirements?.........41
The Hierarchy of Control Systems.........41
Examples of how you can remove a hazard are as follows.........41
Are The Current Controls Adequate?.........42
What Further Action is required to reduce the Risk to an Acceptable Level? ***.........42
Implementation.........43
Monitoring ***.........43

CONTRACTORS AND CREW, APPRAISAL AND MANAGEMENT.........44

INSTRUCTION, TRAINING, INFORMATION AND SUPERVISION.........47

PLAN AND SET STANDARDS.........51

SAFETY REPRESENTATIVES AND SAFETY COMMITTEES REGULATIONS AND THE HEALTH AND SAETY (CONSULTATION WITH EMPLOYEES) REGULATIONS.........51

EMPLOYERS LIABILITY INSURANCE.........52

INFORMATION TO EMPLOYEES.........53

MEASURING PERFORMANCE.........53

A CASE STUDY.........56

WORKING TIME REGULATIONS, TRAVEL AND ACCOMMODATION.........58

REST BREAKS...59
ACCOMMODATION 59
TRAVEL INSURANCE AND FIRST AID.......................................60
ACCIDENT AND INCIDENT REPORTING.......................60
EQUIPMENT...53
DRIVING..54
INDUCTIONS...65
**LOADING/UNLOADING VEHICLES AND
    MANUAL HANDLING**..66
LOCAL CREW..66
MANUAL HANDLING 67
STAGES AND RISERS 67
ELECTRICS...68
WORK AT HEIGHT 68
NOISE..69
   Disposable Ear Plug Fitting Instructions 69
SPECIAL EFFECTS...70
   Strobes..71
   Ultraviolet light...71
   Lasers 71
   Lamps and HMI Lamp Systems 71
   Other Lighting Effects...72
   Smoke, Vapour and Fog Effects..72
Show Stop Procedure...73
Miscellaneous Hazards..74
General Safety Rules..76
Working Environment...77
Walkways, Steps and Stages..78
Tool and Equipment Maintenance....................................78
Personal Protective Equipment..78
Manual Handling, Lifting and Moving...............................79

Electrical Safety 80

SELF-EMPLOYMENT IN THE LIVE MUSIC AND EVENTS INDUSTRY
A Guide for the Self-Employed and those who use the services of the Self-Employed 83

DISCLAIMER 85
    Self-Employment vs PAYE Words of warning
        by Chris Hannam and Nick Cook 85

Draft Freelancer Contract 87
Well? 89
The Limited Company Option 90
A Simple Guide to Self Employment 91
    Interpretation 91

Introduction 92
What is Self-Employment? 93

TEMPLATE CONTRACT TO PROVIDE GOODS AND SERVICES 97

TERMS OF BUSINESS 99

CONTRACTS 103
    The Department for Business, Enterprise & Regulatory Reform 103
        The contract of employment 103
        Employed or self-employed? 103
        Written statement of employment particulars 104
        Variation of contract 104
        Refusal by employee to authorise variation 105
        Breach of contract claims by employees 106
        Breach of contract claims by employers 106
        Constructive unfair dismissal 107

IR 35 – IGNORANCE IS NO DEFENCE 107
IR 56 – GUIDANCE ON EMPLOYMENT STATUS 109
SIMPLIFIED CHECKLIST OF STATUS FACTORS 114

Strong indicators 115
Weak indicators 115
TAX REGULATION – SECTION 660 116
What is Section 660 (s660a)? 116
Insurance 116
Employers' Liability 119
Public Liability 119
Product Liability 120
Professional Indemnity 120
Key Man Cover 120
Business Interruption 120
Goods in Transit 121
Property and Buildings 121
Business assets and equipment (contents cover) 121
THE INCOME TAX (Pay As You Go) (Amendment No2) REGULATIONS 2015 122

ACKNOWLEDGMENTS

Nick Cooke for all his input to the second of these two books and all the production and tour managers who have helped with the first. They include: Craig Duffy, Chris Runciman, Ken Watts, Trigger, Johnny Haskett and a cast of thousands.

HEALTH AND SAFETY MANAGEMENT FOR TOUR AND PRODUCTION MANAGERS

INTRODUCTION

This book is designed to give simple, basic health and safety information to bands, artists, tour, stage and production managers, crew chiefs, heads of department, supervisors or line managers and has been designed as a follow on from *Health And Safety in the Live Music and Event Technical Production Industry.* It will also be of use to local crew companies, especially their crew chiefs and managers.

This book assumes you have both read and have access to *Health And Safety in the Live Music and Event Technical Production Industry* as it contains details of the main common hazards we come across in our line of work and the means of controlling the associated risks.

We are looking at bands doing, gigs, tours, festivals and one-offs but generally speaking, where the band is *not* providing their own production such as PA and lighting.

I mean the kind of gigs where the band travel with a couple of crew in a splitter bus or a van and mini bus or couple of cars with their own back line and the PA and lights are provided by the promoter or venue.

They are the gigs where the venues are usually dismal, dirty, sweat runs down the walls and your feet stick to the floor, you get treated like you're rubbish, half of the PA does not work and lighting is just a few dodgy parcans, there is no hotel and it's a 200 mile drive home after the gig for which you get paid fifty quid or you may be lucky and have a tour bus and be getting paid a bit more but we all know this type of work. If you're the tour manager you will probably be sound engineer and driver as well.

We have all worked at gigs like this, and still have the scars and many memories of slogging up and down motorways and across Europe. Some were unbearably uncomfortable journeys and terrible gigs but some of them were a lot of fun with great shows and we still have the stories we can tell (but perhaps we should not tell them as it may incriminate someone in some way) or you may have had the privilege of being a support act at a larger venue or festival and have experienced the joy of being trampled on by the headline act's management and crew.

This guide will hopefully help you to avoid the health and safety hazards and pit falls that are all too common at this level of touring.

One other important source of information you should be aware of and use is the *Purple Guide.* This is the online replacement to the *Event Safety Guide* published by the Health and Safety Executive. The new edition is published by the Event Industry Forum and is available at: www.thepurpleguide.co.uk

The *Purple Guide* is supported be the Health and Safety Executive, is essential reading, and covers events of all shapes and sizes.

If you really want to know the secret of successful gigs at this level then it's simple; it's all down to the planning because poor planning produces p*** poor product. I don't mean 80% planning in advance and let the rest sort its self out on the day, I mean 101% planning in advance.

Managing health and safety is an integral part of managing your business/tours. You need to do risk assessments to find out about the risks in your workplace, put sensible measures in place to control them, and make sure they stay controlled.

Just the mere mention of the words "health and safety" often conjures up negative images of over-zealous 'jobs-worths', getting in the way of doing business, and creating unnecessary costs. It is easy to see why this is the case, with the media often reporting inaccurate stories about activities being banned on health and safety grounds, or with the words 'health and safety' often being used as a poor excuse when people don't want something to happen. Let's not fall into that trap.

Planning is the key to ensuring your health and safety arrangements really work. It helps you think through the actions you have set out in your policy and work out how they will happen in practice.

Consider:

- what you want to achieve, e.g. how you will ensure that your employees and others are kept healthy and safe at work;
- how you will decide what might cause harm to people and whether you are doing enough or need to do more to prevent that harm;
- how you will prioritise the improvements you may need to make;
- who will be responsible for health and safety tasks, what they should do, when and with what results;
- how you will measure and review whether you have achieved what you set out to do.

Accident Costs

Britain has a relatively good health and safety record yet 1.2 million people suffered from a work-related illness and over 600 000 work place injuries were reported in 2010/11, leading to 26.4 million working days being lost due to work-related injury and illness. In the UK fatal work related accidents occur at a rate of about one a day, a figure that has remained consistent for the past few years.

The cost to British employers was estimated to be £3.1 billion in 2009/10. The Health and Safety Executive (HSE) suggests that £910 million to £3,710 million comes from accidental damage to property and equipment.

Most organisations do not know what accidents and ill-health really cost them in time and money. Few bother to examine costs if and when they investigate accidents and incidents.

In October 2012 the Fee for Intervention (FFI) came into effect with the approval of the Health and Safety (Fees) Regulations 2012. These Regulations have put a duty on the Health and Safety Executive (HSE) to recover its costs for carrying out its regulatory functions from those found to be in material breach of health and safety law rather than from the public purse. The fee is based on the amount of time that an inspector has to spend identifying the material breach, helping businesses to put it right, investigating and taking enforcement action. The rate charged is £124 per hour.

It is often assumed that most accident and incident costs are recoverable through insurance. This is a dangerous and incorrect conception. It is highly unlikely that any insurance will be valid if you breach health and safety legislation much of which is criminal law. You can't insure against breaching criminal law, it's like drinking and driving, and your insurance is not valid if driving under the influence of drugs or alcohol.

The HSE estimates that uninsured losses are ten times the cost of insurance premiums paid with uninsured losses from accidents in smaller firms adding up to £315 per employee, per year.

Uninsured costs can include:

- Lost time
- Sick pay
- Damage or loss of product and raw materials
- Repairs to plant and equipment
- Extra wages, overtime working and temporary labour
- Production delays
- Investigation time

- Fines
- Loss of contracts
- Legal costs
- Accident and ill-health costs can be likened to an iceberg: costs that are recoverable are visible but those that are unrecoverable are hidden below the waterline and are many times greater.

Iceberg of Workplace Injury Costs

Insurance Costs
Covering Injury, ill health, damage

Uninsured Costs
Product and material damage
Plant and building damage
Tool and equipment damage
Legal costs
Expenditure on emergency supplies
Clearing site
Production delays
Overtime working and temporary labour
Investigation time
Supervisor's time diverted
Clerical effort
Fines
Loss of expertise/experience
Loss of reputation
Increased insurance costs

Other key points to consider

- Losing key personnel due to injury or ill-health can be critical to meeting contract deadlines and missing shows.
- In smaller organisations which have little reserve capacity, a serious accident or an incident such as fire can spell the end of the business altogether.

- Loss of business reputation due to accidents and enforcement action can lead to loss of new or repeat business or loss of new investment.
- Accidents can damage workforce morale and affect productivity.
- Serious accidents leading to injury may be rare but minor incidents leading to costly damage are happening much of the time.
- Accident claims invariably mean higher insurance premiums or insurance cover actually being refused.

After all that there often follow civil claims from victims or their family. If you think safety is expensive, try having an accident!

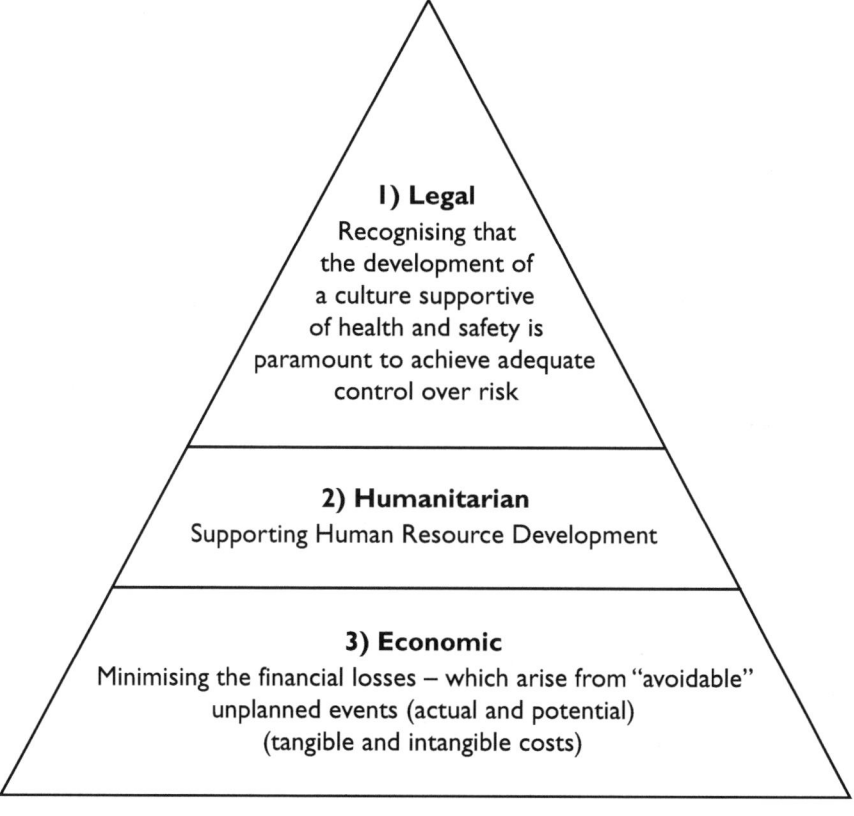

The humane reasons for health and safety is to prevent suffering and maintain quality of life, no-one should be expected to risk life and limb in return for a contract of employment.

The Health and Safety at Work etc Act 1974

The basis of British health and safety law is the *Health and Safety at Work etc Act 1974*. Under this Act of Parliament lies a vast array of regulations to cover just about every health and safety topic imaginable, and one of the most important of these is the *Management of Health and Safety at Work Regulations 1999*.

The Act sets out the general duties which employers have towards employees and members of the public, and employees have to themselves and to each other.

These duties are qualified in the Act by the principle of *'so far as is reasonably practicable'*. In other words, an employer does not have to take measures to avoid or reduce the risk if they are technically impossible or if the time, trouble or cost of the measures would be grossly disproportionate to the risk.

What the law requires here is what good management and common sense would lead employers to do anyway: that is, to look at what the risks are and take sensible measures to tackle them.

The general duties contained in the Health and Safety at Work Act are:

Section 1: States the general purposes of Part 1 of the Act, which are to maintain or improve standards of health and safety at work, to protect other people against risks arising from work activities, to control the storage and use of dangerous substances and to control certain emissions into the air.

Section 2: Contains the duties placed upon employers with regard to their employees. These are outlined more fully below.

Section 3: Places duties on employers and the self-employed to ensure their activities do not endanger anybody (with the self-employed that includes themselves), and to provide information, in certain circumstances, to the public about any potential hazards.

Section 4: Places a duty on those in control of premises, which are non-domestic and used as a place of work, to ensure they do not endanger those who work within them. This extends to plant and substances, means of access and egress as well as to the premises themselves.

Section 6: Places duties on manufacturers, suppliers, designers, importers etc. in relation to articles and substances used at work. Basically they have to research and test them and supply information to users.

Section 7: Places duties upon employees and these are outlined more fully below.

Section 8: Places a duty on everyone not to intentionally or recklessly interfere with or misuse anything provided in the interests of health, safety and welfare.

Section 9: Provides that an employer may not charge his employees for anything done, or equipment provided for health and safety purposes under a relevant statutory provision.

Health and Safety Enforcement

The Health and Safety Executive (HSE) and Local Authorities (LAs) are responsible for enforcing health and safety legislation. Together they ensure duty holders manage the health and safety of their workforce and those affected by their work.

LAs are the principle enforcing authority in retailing, wholesale distribution, warehousing, hotel and catering premises, offices, and the consumer/leisure industries that include entertainment venues, theatres, night clubs, concert halls, arenas, stadiums and festival sites. The HSE is the principal enforcing authority for construction (including stages and temporary structures), agriculture and factories.

LAs are also responsible for issuing Licenses for Licensed Entertainment and alcohol that are required by the Licensing Act 2003.

Powers of the enforcement authorities

Health and safety inspectors may enter your work premises at any time. Remember that work premises can include the homes of home workers.

Usually the inspector will be visiting to carry out a health and safety inspection. However, they could also visit you after an accident that may have been caused by work activities.

They will then be seeking to:

- investigate the causes of the accident
- advise you whether you need to take action to prevent a recurrence
- determine if there has been a breach of health and safety law

Whatever the purpose of the visit, inspectors have the authority to take certain actions, including:

- carrying out examinations and investigations, including taking

measurements, photographs and samples
- taking possession of an article and arranging for it to be dismantled or tested
- seizing and making safe any article or substance that could cause serious personal injury
- requesting information and taking statements from people they think can help an investigation
- inspecting and copying documents

If the inspector considers that you are breaking health and safety law, or your activities give rise to a serious risk, they can:

- issue an informal warning, verbally or in writing
- issue an improvement notice or prohibition notice
- prosecute the company and/or individuals

Prosecutions can lead to huge fines and prison sentences. Much of our health and safety law is Criminal Law but parts also fall under Civil or Common Law in particular the Duty of Care which we all have towards each other. In English tort law, a duty of care is a legal obligation which is imposed on an individual requiring adherence to a standard of reasonable care while performing any acts that could foreseeably harm others. It is the first element that must be established to proceed with an action in a case of negligence. This is easy to prove as there is always a Duty of Care.

Health and safety inspectors can take your attitude into consideration when they are dealing with you, so be nice to them.

When considering whether to prosecute individuals, the HSE consider the management chain and the role played by individual managers and supervisors.

If a manager or supervisor has done everything possible to comply with the law, and has taken all reasonable and normal steps to ensure the health and safety of staff, and any other persons who might be affected, then it is very unlikely that the manager would be considered for prosecution.

Reasonable and normal steps would include: carrying out risk assessments; addressing high risk matters revealed by that assessment; ensuring equipment is regularly checked and maintained; and ensuring that staff understand their own responsibilities in relation to health and safety are properly trained, equipped and competent to fulfil their functions.

LEGAL DUTIES UNDER THE HEALTH AND SAFTY AT WORK ACT

Duties of Employers

Employers are responsible for the health and safety of, and have a duty of care for everyone affected by the business and its activities.

All employers, whatever the size of the business, must:

- prevent risks to health and safety to employees working at the business premises, from home, or at another site, visitors to the business premises such as customers or subcontractors, people at other premises where you're working, such as a venue or festival site, members of the public – even if they're outside the business premises and anyone affected by products and services you design, produce or supply
- ensure that plant and machinery is safe to use, and that safe working practices are set up and followed
- make sure that all materials are handled, stored and used safely
- tell employees about any potential hazards from the work they do, chemicals and other substances used by the firm, and give employees information, instructions, training and supervision as needed
- check that the right work equipment is provided and is properly used and regularly maintained
- consult with employees or their health and safety reps on matters of health and safety
- ensure employees understand and carry out their responsibilities for health and safety, such as following the safety rules the employer has set up
- appoint competent person/s to advise them on health and safety (safety advisors), this may be a person/s employed by the business or an external consultant.

Duties of Employees

- Use any plant, equipment and Personal Protective Equipment (PPE) correctly
  - in accordance with instructions provided.

- Inform their employer directly
  - of anything that may be dangerous
  - of issues that may affect health and safety
- Observe requirements of risk assessments including the use of PPE.
- Report lost, damaged or worn out PPE so it can be immediately replaced.
- Protect themselves and others who may be affected by their actions.
- Not damage or interfere with anything provided in the interests of health and safety
- Take part in the Health and Safety process.
- To cooperate with their employer and help him discharge his health and safety duties

The rights of an employee to work in a safe and healthy environment are given by law, and generally can't be changed or removed by an employer. The most important rights are:

- as far as possible, to have any risks to your health and safety properly controlled
- to be provided, free of charge, with any personal protective and safety equipment
- if you have reasonable concerns about your safety, to stop work and leave your work area, without being disciplined
- to tell your employer about any health and safety concerns you have
- to get in touch with the Health and Safety Executive (HSE) or your local authority if your employer won't listen to your concerns, without being disciplined
- to have rest breaks during the working day, to have time off from work during the working week, and to have annual paid holiday

Duties of the Self-Employed

The self-employed have the duties of both an employer and an employee; this is because they employ themselves.

An event organiser or promoter will often have additional duties including the requirement to comply with any conditions that may be attached to a Premises License issued under the Licensing Act of 2003.

THE HEALTH AND SAFETY POLICY

Under Section 2(3) of the Health and Safety at Work Act 1974:

Every employer shall prepare (and as often as may be appropriate revise) a written statement of his general policy with respect to:

a. The health and safety at work of his employees; and
b. The organisation and arrangements in force for the time being for carrying out that policy, and bring the statement and any revision of it to the notice of all his employees.

The above duty has been modified by the Employers' Health and Safety Policy Statements (Exception) Regulations 1975 to exempt employers, who, for the time being, employ less than five employees, from the need to have a written policy (although not from the need to have a policy as such).

The Health and Safety Policy should contain:

- A General Statements of Intent dated and signed by the owner, chief executive or MD.
- The Organisation, who is responsible for doing what with regard to health and safety.
- The Arrangements. In practice these are often divided into general arrangements (fire procedures, emergency procedures, first-aid facilities, risk assessment arrangements, etc.) which apply to all employees and specific arrangements (how to use certain pieces of equipment, how to handled certain substances, etc.) which only apply to specific employees.

Employers are required to implement the Policy and bring it to the attention of employees.

CULTURE

There is no single definition of 'a safety culture'. It is a term best used to describe the way in which safety is managed in the workplace, and often reflects "the attitudes, beliefs, perceptions and values that employees share in relation to safety".

To make your health and safety policy effective employers need to get their staff involved and **committed**. This is often referred to as a 'positive health and safety culture'.

The four 'Cs' of positive health and safety culture

1. **Competence**: recruitment, training and advisory support.

- A competent person is someone who has the skill, experience, knowledge and training to assess the risks arising from work activities and to work safely. They also know their own limitations and know how, when and where to seek information and advice if required.

2. **Control**: allocating responsibilities, securing commitment, instruction and supervision.
   - Lead by example: demonstrate your commitment and provide clear direction – let everyone know health and safety is important.
   - Identify people responsible for particular health and safety jobs – especially where special expertise is called for, e.g. doing risk assessments, operating equipment.
   - Ensure that managers, supervisors and crew chiefs understand their responsibilities and have the time and resources to carry them out.
   - Ensure everyone knows what they must do and how they will be held accountable – set objectives.

3. **Co-operation**: between individuals and groups.
   - Chair your health and safety committee – if you have one. Consult your staff and their representatives.
   - Involve staff in planning and reviewing performance, writing procedures and solving problems.
   - Co-ordinate and co-operate with your contractors on site.

4. **Communication**: spoken, written and visible.
   - Provide information about hazards, risks and preventive measures to employees and contractors working on your premises.
   - Discuss health and safety regularly.
   - Be 'visible' on health and safety.

A safety culture is one in which safety is regarded by everyone as being an issue which concerns everyone. As a result, safety rules are understood and adhered to; negative and macho attitudes to safety ('we could not work if we followed health and safety regulations' / 'hard hats are for wimps') go out of the window and accidents and near-miss incidents are reported and investigated quickly and thoroughly.

Strong safety cultures can be observed in many high-risk industries, such as offshore drilling installations.

The benefits of the safety culture to the organisation as a whole extend beyond a fall in the number of accidents. Studies have shown that companies demonstrating strong safety cultures also show improvements in performance, quality standards and staff morale.

The safety culture of an organisation is the product of individual and group values, attitudes, perceptions, competencies and patterns of behaviour that determine the commitment to, and the style and proficiency of, an organisation's health and safety management that must exist at all levels and in all departments and not just 'on-site'.

Organisations with a positive safety culture are characterised by communications founded on mutual trust, by shared perceptions of the importance of safety and by confidence in the efficacy of preventative measures.

Safety culture is not a difficult idea, but it is usually described in terms of concepts such as 'trust', values' and 'attitudes'. It can be difficult to describe what these mean, but you can judge whether a company has a good safety culture from what its employees actually do rather than what they say.

The symptoms of a poor health and safety cultural include:

- Widespread, routine procedural violations;
- Failures of compliance with health and safety systems;
- Poor communication;
- Management decisions that put production or cost before safety.

These conditions can be difficult to detect because a poor culture not only contributes to their occurrence, it also means that people may be inclined to hide or cover-up violations and unsafe practices. However, it is easy to detect the fourth symptom, we often see situations whereby it is obvious that some people in the company wish to improve matters but as soon busy work periods start safety is suspended to such a level that more violations often take place.

The approach your company takes to health and safety in the workplace will have a significant impact on the success of your policy. Many companies take a purely legalistic approach to the subject; they assume that legal minimum standards are acceptable and do nothing over and above what the law requires.

This approach deserves criticism in that, through its own indifference to safety issues, this type of company is indirectly encouraging its employees to disrespect safety rules and safe working practices. Companies which set high standards in health and safety management can demonstrate the existence of a safety 'culture' in their workplaces. This starts at base, in the office, warehouse or workshops. In many instances the 'core business' activities are out on site away from the office or warehouse, so it is often considered that the office and warehouse are drains on resources. But for health and safety purposes your 'culture' must start here: in the office and warehouse. Cultural factors influence all aspects of the running of an organisation including health and safety. Every organisation has its own unique culture or set of cultures, which develop and grow over time.

Through effective safety management it is possible to encourage and promote the development and growth of a positive safety culture in your workplace. Like it or not, people are like sheep.

New employees joining a business with no safety culture will adopt the attitude that Health and Safety is unimportant or to be avoided. Those who join a business with a strong safety culture will quickly follow and health and safety will be very high on their agendas.

THE MANAGEMENT OF HEALTH AND SAFETY AT WORK REGULATIONS

This is probably the most important regulation that falls under the Health and Safety at Work Act. The Management Regulations make the assessment of risks a cornerstone of UK health and safety requirements. Employers with five or more employees (including directors, partners and the self-employed, need to record the significant findings of a risk assessment – it is not necessary to record risk assessments for trivial or insignificant risks.

These regulations also make it a legal requirement for employers to "manage" safety in a similar manner as you might manage the financial aspects of a business, so you have a auditable safety management system in place that includes appointing competent persons to advise and assist in these duties in the same way as you would appoint an accountant to help and advice on financial matters. In addition employers also need to:

- make arrangements for implementing the health and safety measures

identified as necessary by risk assessments. This will cover planning (setting priorities), organisation (putting in place the structure to implement the measures), control (ensuring that safety decisions are being implemented as planned), and monitoring and review (keeping tabs on preventive and protective measures and striving for progressive improvement in health and safety performance).
- appoint people with sufficient knowledge, skills, experience and training to help them to implement these arrangements (Safety Advisors)
- set up emergency procedures and provide information about them to employees
- provide clear information, supervision and training for employees and ensure that suitably competent people are appointed who are capable of carrying out the tasks entrusted to them
- work together with any other employer(s) operating from the same workplace, sharing information on the risks that other staff may be exposed to, e.g. on site or at a venue for an event or tour, cleaning, catering or maintenance contractors
- take particular account of risks to new and expectant mothers.

PLAN, DO, CHECK, ACT	Conventional health and safety management	Process safety
PLAN	Determine and describe how you manage health and safety in your business (your legally required policy) and plan to make it happen in practice (how you will implement the policy)	Define and communicate acceptable performance and resources needed
DO	Prioritise and control your risks – consult your employees and provide training and information. Organise for health and safety. Implement your plan.	Identify and assess risks/ Identify controls Record and maintain process safety knowledge Implement and manage control measure
CHECK	Measure performance (monitor before events, investigate after events) Measure how you are doing and investigate the causes of any accidents, incidents or near-misses.	Measure and review performance Learn from measurements and findings of investigations

PLAN, DO, CHECK, ACT	Conventional health and safety management	Process safety
ACT	Review performance Act on lessons learned	Learn from experience and take action on lessons learned.

The elements of the safety management process (see table above) are simply described by their necessary outcomes.

PLAN

Think about where you are now and where you need to be.

Say what you want to achieve, who will be responsible for what, how you will achieve your aims, and how you will measure your success. You may need to write down this policy and your plan to deliver it.

Decide how you will measure performance. Think about ways to do this that go beyond looking at accident figures; look for leading indicators as well as lagging indicators. These are also called active and reactive indicators.

Consider fire and other emergencies. Co-operate with anyone who shares your workplace and co-ordinate plans with them.

Remember to plan for changes and identify any specific legal requirements that apply to you.

DO

Identify your risk profile. Assess the risks, identify what could cause harm in the workplace, who it could harm and how, and what you will do to manage the risk.

Decide what the priorities are and identify the biggest risks.

Organise your activities to deliver your plan

In particular, aim to:

Involve workers and communicate, so that everyone is clear on what is needed and can discuss issues – develop positive attitudes and behaviours.

Provide adequate resources, including competent advice where needed.

Implement your plan. Decide on the preventive and protective measures needed and put them in place.

Provide the right tools and equipment to do the job and keep them maintained.

Train and instruct, to ensure everyone is competent to carry out their work.

Supervise to make sure that arrangements are followed.

CHECK

Measure your performance. Make sure that your plan has been implemented – 'paperwork' on its own is not a good performance measure.

Assess how well the risks are being controlled and if you are achieving your aims. In some circumstances formal audits may be useful.

Investigate the causes of accidents, incidents or near misses

ACT

Review your performance. Learn from accidents and incidents, ill-health data, errors and relevant experience, including from other organisations.

Revisit plans, policy documents and risk assessments to see if they need updating.

Take action on lessons learned, including from audit and inspection reports

Plan, Do, Check, Act should not be seen as a once-and-for-all action: You may need to go round the cycle more than once, particularly when:

- starting out;
- developing a new process, product or service; or
- implementing any change

These elements can all be expanded, but are seen as the minimum consistent with current legal obligations and the desire to minimise loss.

SAFE SYSTEMS OF WORK (SSoW)
Definition:

A formal procedure which results from systematic examination of a task in order to identify all the hazards. It defines safe methods to ensure that hazards are eliminated or risks minimised.

Hazard and Risk

A **hazard** is anything with the potential to cause harm.
A **risk** is the likelihood of harm and the seriousness of the consequences

Legislation

HASAWA Section 2 (2) (a) requires employers to: Provide and maintain plant and systems of work that are, so far as is reasonably practicable, safe and without risks to health.

The term "so far as is reasonably practicable" means that the degree of risk in a particular situation can be balanced against the time, trouble, cost and physical difficulty of taking measures to avoid the risk. If these resources are so disproportionate to the risk that it would be unreasonable to expect any employer to have to incur them to prevent it, the employer is not obliged to do so unless there is a specific requirement that he does.

The greater the risk, the more likely it is that it is reasonable to go to very substantial expense, time, trouble and invention to reduce it. But if the consequences and extent of a risk are small, insistence on great expense would not be considered reasonable.

It is important to remember that the judgement is an objective one and the size or financial position of the employer is immaterial.

Self-employed persons have a general duty in the Health and Safety at Work Act to conduct their undertakings in a way that ensures, so far as is reasonably practicable, that they, and any others affected by what they do, are not exposed to health and safety risks.

Components of a Safe System

A safe system of work combines materials, people, plant, equipment, task and environment.

It must have logical well-thought out approach.

It should fully identify and document all the hazards, safety precautions and safe working practices associated with all activities performed by employees.

When is a SSoW required?

Many hazards are clearly recognisable and can be overcome by physically separating people from them e.g. by using guarding on machinery, by filling in a large hole in the ground or erecting a fence around hazardous operations and work sites.

A SSoW is needed when hazards cannot be physically eliminated and some element of risk remains.

Remember non-routine work as well as normal operations.

Managers and supervisors have a major part to play in helping to establish SSoW.

Implementation

Safe systems of work must be communicated properly, understood by employees and applied correctly.

Managers and supervisors must know that they should implement and maintain the system of work.

Ensure adequate training is carried out for employees.

Stress the need to avoid short cuts – part of the system should be to stop work when faced with an unexpected problem until a safe solution can be found.

METHOD STATEMENTS, PERMITS TO WORK AND RISK ASSESSMENTS

Method Statements

A work method statement is simply a written "safe system of work"; a document that details the way a work task or process is to be completed.

The method statement should outline the hazards involved and include a step by step guide on how to do the job safely. The method statement must also detail which control measures have been introduced to ensure the safety of anyone who is affected by the task or process. Manufacturers' instructions (that should be available to all users of work equipment) are one example of a Method Statement; another example is a recipe in a cookery book or the instructions on how to assemble a model aircraft kit or a piece of flat packed furniture. Method statements contain safety information and instructions but have no legal status.

Permits to Work

Where proposed work is identified as having a high risk, strict controls are required. The work must be carried out against previously agreed safety procedures, a 'permit-to-work' system. Permits to work are legal documents.

The permit-to-work is a documented procedure that authorises certain people to carry out specific work within a specified time frame at a specified place.

It sets out the precautions required to complete the work safely, based on a risk assessment.

It describes what work will be done and how it will be done; the latter can be detailed in a 'method statement'.

The permit-to-work requires declarations from both the people authorising the work and those carrying out the work.

Permits to work are often required for hot work such as welding, disk cutting, work at height, work in confined spaces, live electrical work, use of certain chemicals, etc and are often a requirement at many venues. Managers and supervisors should always check to see if they are required and if so obtain the permit for use by staff.

The essential elements of a PTW system are:

- Full explanation of the hazards involved to the workforce.
- The work to be carried out is properly detailed and understood by both sides.
- The area in which the work to be carried out is properly detailed and understood by both sides.
- The area is which the work is to be carried out is clearly identified and made safe, or the hazards are highlighted.
- The operatives must sign the permit to say that they fully understand the work that is to be carried out, and the hazards and potential risks to be faced.
- When the work is finished, the operatives must sign off the permit to say that they have completed the specified work and left the operation in a suitable state.

Risk Assessments

Employers have a duty to carry out and record written risk assessments if they employ five or more persons; this includes employers, directors, partners, etc. as well as all crew members. It is almost certain that your touring party with exceed five persons so risk assessments are considered an essential legal requirement.

Risk assessment is the main method we now use to identify hazards and introduce methods of controlling risk so it is important that for a tour, stage and production managers, etc. have a clear understanding as to their implementation and use.

We looked at the basic principles of risk assessment in the previous book in this series. Let's now look at risk assessments in more detail. First note that risk assessments can be recorded in any format. There are hundreds of different types of risk assessment forms, as long as all the required information is included they are all correct.

One of the most important ways to help in establishing SSoW is to carry out and implement to outcomes from risk assessments.

A risk assessment is a systematic method of looking at work activities, considering what could go wrong, and deciding on suitable control measures to prevent loss, damage or injury in the workplace. The assessment should include the controls required to eliminate, reduce or minimise the risks.

Risk assessments are a fundamental requirement for businesses. If an employer, manager or supervisor does not know, or appreciate where the risks are, they are putting themselves, employees and customers of the organisation in danger as well as breaching criminal law.

Employers, managers and supervisors must look at all work activities that could cause harm in order to decide whether they are doing enough to meet their legal obligations.

This is a minimum requirement. If it is reasonably practicable to do so, employers, managers and supervisors should consider doing more than the legal minimum to meet legal requirements.

The aim should always be to reduce the risks as much as is 'reasonably practicable'.

As we have already stated, 'Reasonably practicable' is a legal term that means you must balance the cost of steps that they could take to reduce a risk against the degree of risk presented.

When reckoning costs, the time, trouble and effort required should be included and not just the financial cost.

The results of risk assessments must be communicated to employees so they know the procedures that must be followed; this will usually be a job for managers and supervisors.

Risk assessment should not just a bureaucratic task that has to be

done to avoid falling foul of the law, it is a vital practical tool for:
- identifying hazards
- controlling risk
- making decisions on priorities

Having carried out and implemented our risk assessment it then remains to monitor the operation or hazard to see that all controls are working; if they are not we need to revisit the assessment again.

If needs be, even making a quick assessment record on the 'back of a cigarette packet' is quite acceptable; it at least shows you were trying and adapting to changes in circumstances site and conditions as they arose. Whatever method is chosen, the following points marked *** must be included:

Date of Assessment
Name the Person Making the Assessment
Name the job or operation to be assessed (if applicable, if not, give a brief job description)

Identify the Hazards *
These hazards may include:
- Fire
- Chemicals
- Vehicles or plant
- Moving machinery parts
- Falls (falls from heights, falls at the same level and falls into holes)
- Noise
- Poor light
- Slips and trips
- Weather
- Manual handling
- Electricity
- Work Hours
- Stress
- Aggressive or violent people
- Crowds

Check manufacturers' instructions or data sheets for chemicals and equipment as they can be very helpful in explaining the hazards and putting them in their true perspective.

- Look back at your accident and ill-health records – these often help to identify the less obvious hazards.
- Take account of non-routine operations (e.g. maintenance, cleaning operations or changes in production cycles).
- Remember to think about long-term hazards to health (eg high levels of noise or exposure to harmful substances).

Ask your employees what they think the hazards are, as they may notice things that are not obvious to you and may have some good ideas on how to control the risks.

You will almost certainly find there is more than one hazard associated with each work activity so you may need to complete several assessments to cater for each hazard.

Prioritise and list them in order of highest risk, then it will be possible to carry out a separate assessment for each hazard you have found, starting with the most obvious or serious risk. It is a common mistake to try and assess all the hazards in one assessment; it's risk assessments not risk assessment.

List those at risk and approximate numbers *** (List these as groups not by individual name)

These may include:

- Your own staff
- Other contractors and performers
- Stewards
- Members of the public

For each hazard you need to be clear about who might be harmed – it will help you identify the best way of controlling the risk. That doesn't mean listing everyone by name, but rather identifying groups of people (e.g. people working in the storeroom or passers-by).

Some workers may have particular requirements, e.g. new and young workers, migrant workers, new or expectant mothers, people with disabilities, temporary workers, contractors, homeworkers and lone workers.

Think about people who might not be in the workplace all the time, such as visitors, contractors and maintenance workers.

Take members of the public into account if they could be harmed by your work activities.

If you share a workplace with another business, consider how your work affects others and how their work affects you and your workers. Talk to each other and make sure controls are in place.

Ask your workers if there is anyone you may have missed.

Having identified the hazards, you then have to decide how likely it is that harm will occur, i.e. the level of risk and what to do about it. Risk is a part of everyday life and you are not expected to eliminate all risks. What you must do is make sure you know about the main risks and the things you need to do to manage them responsibly.

HSE Guidance states that your risk assessment should only include what you could reasonably be expected to know – you are not expected to anticipate unforeseeable risks but things may in future get a difficult as the High Court and Court of Appeal have decided that if an employee removes the safety guard from a machine while it is running (against instruction) to clean the machine and subsequently has an accident then the employer should have foreseen that accident and should have carried out a risk assessment to cover the foolish actions of an employee! Sometimes are law is an ass and this verdict has caused waves among many safety professionals.

What is the likelihood of an accident?

Impossible, remote, possible, probable or likely?

(Consider what the likelihood will be *without any* controls in place whatsoever. Don't make the mistake of assuming that some controls are already in place).

What could be the worst possible outcome of an accident?

(Consider what the outcome would be *without any* controls in place whatsoever, and don't make the mistake of assuming that some controls are already in place).

It may be:

- Equipment Damage - No Injury
- Trivial Injury
- Minor Injury
- Major Injury
- Fatal Injury

Risk Class

The above information can now help us to class the risk as High, Moderate, Minor or Acceptable.

Risk = Hazard Severity x Likelihood of Occurrence (x Number of People Exposed).

A Hazard Index Table can be produced:

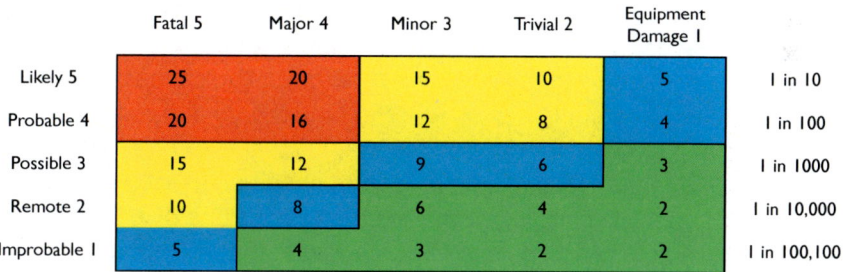

Having evaluated and classed the risk we can now look at ways of controlling the risk.

Information

List here the current information available on the hazards. You will have to do some research to obtain the information required that will help identify the appropriate methods of controlling the risks. Remember, your controls must meet the standards set by legal requirement so you will have to research documents and publications including:

- Approved Codes of Practice
- HSE Guidance
- Safety Data Sheets
- Statutory Regulations
- Manufacturer's Instructions

- Company Safety Rules or Policy
- British/GEN Standards
- Codes of Practice
- Industry Best Practice
- Personal Experience

This is another area where many people go wrong; they simply fail to do the research. It may seem an incredible amount of work but it's not really that bad.

Researching the regulations and guidance are a vital part of risk assessment and I cannot over stress the importance of the research to be included as a suitable and sufficient (adequate) risk assessment. Do not skip on this as the guidance will advise you as to the controls that you will need to implement. Please don't just follow your own judgement.

Part of the work of the Health and Safety Executive is accident prevention and producing information in the form of guidance documents and Approved Codes of Practice (ACoPs) on hazards and regulations.

An Approved Code of Practice is important in that it has a special legal status. If you are prosecuted for a breach of health and safety law, and it is proved that you did not follow the relevant provisions of an Approved Code of Practice, you would need to demonstrate that you have complied with the law in some other way that is at least equal to or exceeds the requirements of the ACoP or a Court would find you at fault.

Guidance documents describe ways of complying with the regulations. Guidance does not have the special legal status associated with ACoPs, however following the guidance will help you to comply with the Regulations and give advice on good practice.

Following guidance is not compulsory and organisations are free to take other action. However, if you follow the guidance you would normally be doing enough to comply with the law.

Guidance and ACoPS published by the HSE are available for free down load from the HSE web site or HSE Books. (www.hse.gov.uk or books.hse.gov.uk)

Current Controls ***

What are your present systems for controlling the risk? Controls will fit into one of the following groups:

- Architectural
- Managerial or
- Physical

An example of an architectural control is the safety refuge in a loading bay or constructing a building from stone, concrete and metal (instead of wood) to prevent fire. An example of a managerial control is the employer or production manager giving an instruction or warnings or it may be a safety sign and a physical control maybe something like a portable loading ramp.

Do your current controls meet the standards set by legal requirement?

What is in place right now? Do not list what you intend to do in the future, only what is in place now.

The next common mistake is to assume that some things are already in place to control the risk; you probably have little or nothing in place right now.

These 'controls' may include any of the following. Remember, the first step in controlling a risk is to try to remove the hazard.

The Hierarchy of Control Systems

- Remove the hazard (the best option if it's possible to do so)
- Access controls to the work area
- Training, qualifications, supervision and instruction
- Written safe systems of work such as method statements and permits to work
- Provision of suitable work equipment
- Testing, inspecting and certification of plant and equipment
- Structural calculations
- Warning signs (are used to back up other controls; they are not a control in their own right).
- Personal protective equipment or clothing (very much a last resort)

Examples of how you can remove a hazard are as follows:

- by replacing a hazardous chemical with a safer one
- by engineering controls such as putting a generator in a sound proofed container to remove a noise hazard
- by replacing a dangerous operation with a safer option
- by mechanising a manual handling operation
- by routing leads and cables to prevent a trip hazard
- separation of vehicles, plant and machines from people
- by filling in or covering a hole in the ground
- by turning off the power before working on electrical equipment

Look at what you're already doing and the control measures you already have in place. Ask yourself:

- Can I get rid of the hazard altogether?
- If not, how can I control the risks so that harm is unlikely?

Some practical steps you could take include:

- trying a less risky option;
- preventing access to the hazards;
- organising your work to reduce exposure to the hazard;
- issuing protective equipment;
- providing welfare facilities such as first aid and washing facilities;
- involving and consulting with workers.

It is important to remember that first aid provision is not a method of controlling risk (it's what we do to patch injured people up) so don't list first aid provision as a method of controlling risk. This is a fundamental mistake we see time and time again.

Are The Current Controls Adequate?

Yes or No? If the answer is Yes, move on to the section on Monitoring If the answer is No:

What Further Action is Required to Reduce the Risk to an Acceptable Level? ***

List what you need to do to reduce the risk to an acceptable level. The law says you should first of all try to remove the risk but if this is not possible then the next best option should be used. If the risk is classed as 'high' you *can't* take cost into consideration when considering what control systems may be suitable.

Always remember: if at all possible our first option as a 'control system' is to always try and remove the hazard or replace it with a safer alternative and the last option we should consider is the use of personal protective equipment [PPE] (and clothing).

Give yourself a target date to put any new controls into practice and name the person responsible for doing this. Record all this information on the assessment sheet.

Remember, risk assessment is about what is happening in the workplace *not what you think is happening*.

Implementation***

I see so many situations where completed risk assessments are just filed away and only see the light of day when clients request copies of risk assessments from their vendors. This is not the correct use of risk assessments; they should be provided to all members of your staff or crew who are carrying out the operations covered by each assessment so they know exactly what controls they need to put in place. It's not rocket science!

Monitoring ***

This is one of the most important parts of the process. You must monitor your control systems to see that they are working adequately to control the risks. If they are not working you should review your assessment.

Name the person responsible for monitoring the controls and reviewing the assessment. Note how frequently you are going to monitor and list the dates or even the times if necessary.

Some operations will need to be monitored more frequently than others but assessments should always be reviewed annually or when work, materials, practices or circumstances otherwise change.

Managers, supervisors, crew bosses and heads of departments provide local leadership and manage the completion of tasks. Management and supervision includes setting a good example and making sure that operatives work safely – this uses the same skills as checking that the quality of work is acceptable and that production is progressing to plan.

Monitoring is a line management responsibility and can be supplemented by a health and safety advisor's visits. Monitoring is more proactive and structured than supervision. Both follow simple systems to sample, check and report on health and safety performance at regular intervals.

The whole point about these assessments is that they should not just be a 'paper exercise'.

To be effective all staff must be involved and the controls continually monitored to see that they are working; this is part of our 'health and safety culture' in action. Remember, risk assessment is a means to an end; it is not the end itself.

CONTRACTORS AND CREW, APPRAISAL AND MANAGEMENT

This still comes as a shock to some people but legally you cannot appoint contractors and simply "let them get on with it". An employer or business (the client) is responsible for the contractors they appoint. You can contract work out but not pass on liability.

Employers need to satisfy themselves that contractors are competent (i.e. they have sufficient skills and knowledge) to do the job safely and without risks to health and safety. The degree of competence required will depend on the work to be done. Make sure contractors know and understand what performance you expect. Explain your health and safety arrangements to them. Show them your procedures, permit systems, health and safety policy statement and make sure they understand and will act in accordance with it.

Your first responsibility is to ensure all crew members you appoint are competent. The terms 'competent' and 'competency' appear regularly in Health & Safety Regulations and law. Competency is a combination of knowledge, skill and experience. Perhaps the best definition I can give is "someone who has an awareness of the limitations of their own experience and knowledge, who has an understanding of current best practice, who has a willingness and ability to supplement existing experience and knowledge, who has access to specific applied knowledge and skills of appropriately qualified specialists. As far as an employer is concerned, it is his obligation to ensure that the person he chooses for a particular job or task has been adequately trained and is 'competent'.

More complicated and technical situations will require the competent person to have a higher level of knowledge and experience and will require specific applied knowledge and skills which can be only offered by appropriately qualified specialists.

Another very good definition of competence is as follows.

A person who can demonstrate that they have sufficient professional or technical training, knowledge, actual experience, and authority* to enable them to:

- carry out their assigned duties at the level of responsibility allocated to them;
- understand any potential hazards related to the work (or equipment) under consideration;
- detect any technical defects or omissions in that work (or equipment), recognise any implications for health and safety caused by those defects or omissions, and be able to specify any remedial action to mitigate those implications.

*Note: "authority" here means delegated authority to the individual by his employer to carry out a certain function or duty.

Another HSE definition of a competent person is ... "where he has sufficient training and experience or knowledge and other qualities to enable him properly to undertake the measures".

Competence can be described as the combination of training, skills, experience and knowledge that a person has, their ability to apply them to perform a task safely, the ability and willingness and ability to increase experience and knowledge and their ability to know the limitations of their own experience and knowledge.

Other factors, such as attitude and physical ability, can also affect someone's competence.

As far as our industry is concerned, it is perhaps in this area that quality, competence and health and safety are linked most closely. You need to use investigative means to ensure the health and safety competence of the staff you intend to appoint as you are responsible for their safety and must provide them with a safe system of work, a safe place of work and safe work equipment. Ultimately it is the employer who is responsible for deciding if a person or company is competent. That can be quite a daunting prospect and not something you want to get correct especially if things have already gone wrong. The only consolation then is to know that only the courts can decide if the person you appointed was in fact competent. The biggest mistake, and the one most often seen in our industry, is employers who select staff by their experience and "can do attitude" alone. A number of factors including training and qualifications should be considered, not just experience and deciding if they have a "can do attitude".

The latter can be dangerous as staff may take on activities far beyond their capabilities in order to please a client – particularly when last minute changes are made to specifications and schedules. Such changes should always be resisted and avoided by proper advance planning, so we must now go further and assess staff for their competence and that includes training, knowledge, experience, knowing their own limitations together with knowing where and how to seek and obtain further information.

The advice is to have a written set of procedures for selecting staff; this may include one or more of the following techniques:

- Pre-qualification questionnaire (best option)
- Formal or informal interview
- Checks on records of training, experience and qualifications, including safety passport schemes that are highly recommended for all freelance crew who travel from job to job as they save so much time and money by eradicating the need for additional training.
- CVs and references
- Recommendation and reputation
- Observation and previous experience of working with that person
- Health and fitness checks if these are felt necessary, or the nature of the work dictates.

Advice on fitness and health checks can be obtained from the HSE Employment Medical Advisory Service (EMAS).

At the same time as making these checks you should also check on prospective crew member holding the required and current Public/Employers Liability insurance and if required, a suitable driving licence, a scan or photocopy of which should kept on file together with a scan/photocopy of their passport (if travelling outside the UK) and contact details of next of kin in case of emergency.

As already noted, it's also a sad fact that in our industry the selection of suppliers/providers/contractors and staff is primarily based on a network of informal personal contacts and 'experience' is considered to be the primary proof of competence at all levels (from management to crew). There is little requirement to provide evidence of competency.

This is a situation that *must* change!

Once crew have been appointed they should be given a copy of the Health and Safety Policy as covered above with the instruction they should read and understand it. It's a good plan to get them to sign to say they have received, read and understand the policy. The Policy may be provided electronically/online. The policy ensures everyone is singing from the same song sheet and it is an important legal document.

Remember to request information from contractors and staff and assess their competence *BEFORE* they are appointed. The best method is to ask for the information with their quote. The quotes of those not supplying the information or unsatisfactory information should be rejected. For smaller events or tours it will usually fall back to the tour manager to fulfil these duties.

So having selected our staff and contractors using an auditable selection process and finally appointed them we now have to manage them.

Clients and contractors need to consider what information should be passed between them and agree appropriate ways to make sure this is done. They need to exchange clear information about the risks arising from their operations, including relevant safety rules and procedures, and procedures for dealing with emergencies. This exchange of information should include details of any risks that other parties could not reasonably be expected to know about. The information must be specific to the work. On site inductions are one method of conveying this information.

In other words, you must talk to one another and then GET IT IN WRITING!

INSTRUCTION, TRAINING, INFORMATION AND SUPERVISION

We have already looked at method statements, permits to work and risk assessments as part of our safe systems of work, but SsoW also includes instruction, training, information and supervision. The Health and Safety at Work etc Act 1974 requires all employers to provide whatever information, instruction, training and supervision as is necessary to ensure, so far as is reasonably practicable, the health and safety at work of their employees and this duty will fall to managers, crew chiefs and supervisors who have a vital role in assisting in the delivery of instruction, information, training and supervision of your crew at all times.

This is expanded by the Management of Health and Safety at Work Regulations 1999, which identify situations where health and safety training is particularly important, e.g. when people start work, on exposure to new or increased risks and where existing skills may have become rusty or need updating.

Employers must provide training during working hours and not at the expense of their employees. Special arrangements may be needed for part-timers or shift workers.

Employers should keep records of training and qualifications in the employees personnel file together with contact details including that of the next of kin in case of emergency and any relevant health details such as heart or back problems, epilepsy, asthma and diabetes. This information must be kept confidential to comply with the Data Protection Act.

On starting in a new job or work on a new or unfamiliar site or venue, managers and supervisors must ensure that all employees (and the self-employed) are given a short induction where they will be made aware of the following:

The induction should clearly explain:

- The commitment of management to health and safety
- Details of the project
- The name of the person who organises health and safety procedures on site, and how to contact them
- Arrangements for consulting and involving workers on health and safety
- Site-specific health and safety risks
- Arrangements for protective equipment, including what is needed, where to find it and how to use it
- Arrangements for first aid and the location of toilets, washing and canteen facilities

- All emergency exits and means of escape.
- The emergency assembly point/s.
- Fire alarm positions.
- Fire points (fire-fighting equipment such as extinguishers, hose reels, and fire blankets).
- Welfare facilities including toilets, drinking water, canteen or catering facilities, cloakrooms, etc.
- First aid facilities.
- First aiders and fire wardens.
- Location of the accident book and the reporting arrangements.
- Speed limits for vehicles, traffic routes and parking areas.

This is the provision of information.

Everyone is expected to cooperate with this procedure. They may also be required to attend and take part in any safety meetings, updates and briefings.

As soon as possible after starting work all employees should undergo:

a. Basic fire safety training

b. Manual handling training

c. Basic electrical safety training

d. Noise at work training

e. Information on safety signs

This is where safety passports come in. They prove the holder has already received such basic training and it does not need to be repeated but managers and supervisor are ideally placed to provide some basic training such as use of ear protection, fire and emergency procedures, information on safety signs and care and use of PPE. This can be given informally in the form of "tool box talks" in the workplace.

Toolbox talks are short discussions or presentations by supervisors and managers to the employees. They generally last no longer than ten to 15 minutes. Often participants gather around the project tool box, hence the name.

A toolbox talk is focused on one specific topic and addresses it in simple terms. A toolbox talk provides an opportunity for a supervisor or manager to emphasise the importance of a particular issue or procedure, and for staff to ask questions or make serious comments.

If tool box talks are given, managers and supervisors should provide details of the content of the talk and a list of the employees who attended; this information is added to the employees training record held by the company.

A few employees should be selected to undergo:

   a. First Aid at Work Certificate course or Emergency First Aid at Work Certificate course
   b. Fire Wardens Course (if required).

Any specific skill training is in addition to safety training.

You must provide an adequate and appropriate level of supervision for your workers: supervisors, managers and crew chiefs need to know what you expect from them in terms of health and safety. They need to understand your health and safety policy, where they fit in, and how you want health and safety managed.

Managers, supervisors and crew chiefs may need training in the specific hazards of your processes and how you expect the risks to be controlled.

New, inexperienced or young people, as well as those whose first language is not English, are very likely to need more supervision than others. Make sure workers know how to raise concerns and supervisors are familiar with the possible problems due to unfamiliarity, inexperience and communication difficulties.

Supervisors need to ensure that workers in their charge understand risks associated with the work environment and measures to control them.

Supervisors will need to make sure the control measures to protect against risk are up to date and are being properly used, maintained and monitored.

Make sure you have arrangements in place to check the work of contractors is being done as agreed.

Effective supervision can help you monitor the effectiveness of the training that people have received, and whether employees have the necessary capacity and competence to do the job.

PLAN AND SET STANDARDS

Planning is the key to ensuring that your health and safety efforts really work.

Planning for health and safety involves setting objectives, identifying hazards, assessing risks, implementing standards of performance and developing a positive culture. It is often useful to record your plans in writing. Your planning should provide for:

- identifying hazards and assessing risks, and deciding how they can be eliminated or controlled;
- complying with the health and safety laws that apply to your business;
- agreeing health and safety targets with managers and supervisors;
- a purchasing and supply policy which takes health and safety into account;
- design of tasks, processes, equipment, products and services, safe systems of work;
- procedures to deal with serious and imminent danger;
- co-operation with neighbours, and/or subcontractors;
- setting standards against which performance can be measured.

SAFETY REPRESENTATIVES AND SAFETY COMMITTEES REGULATIONS AND THE HEALTH AND SAETY (CONSULTATION WITH EMPLOYEES) REGULATIONS

By law, employers must consult all of their employees on health and safety matters. Where safety representatives have been appointed by a trade union, these may represent the employees in consultations on health and safety with the employer. Consulting employees on health and safety matters is an important way to create and maintain a safe and healthy working environment.

Companies without trade unions or safety representatives will often form a safety committee where safety is planned and discussed on a regular basis.

Employees from all departments and all levels should be represented on these committees.

By consulting employees, an employer should motivate staff and make them aware of health and safety issues. It has been statistically proven that by doing this organisations can become more efficient and reduce the number of accidents and work-related illnesses. Staff who are involved in and are aware of the safety process are far more to embrace and support the health and safety than those who are not involved.

EMPLOYERS LIABILITY INSURANCE

Employers are responsible for the health and safety of their employees while they are at work. Your employees may be injured at work or they, or your former employees, may become ill as a result of their work while in your employment. They might try to claim compensation from you if they believe you are responsible. The Employers' Liability (Compulsory Insurance) Act 1969 ensures that you have at least a minimum level of insurance cover against any such claims.

Employers' liability insurance will enable you to meet the cost of compensation for your employees' injuries or illness whether they are caused on or off site. However, any injuries and illness relating to motor accidents that occur while your employees are working for you may be covered separately by your motor insurance.

You must use an authorised insurer. If you do not, you may be breaking the law. You should check that your insurer is authorised before you take out employers' liability insurance.

You must be insured for at least £5 million. However, you should look carefully at your risks and liabilities and consider whether you need insurance cover of more than £5 million. In practice, most insurers offer cover of at least £10 million.

If your business is part of a group, a policy for employers' liability insurance can be taken out for the group as a whole. In this case, the group as a whole, including subsidiary companies, must have cover of at least £5 million.

You can have more than one policy for employers' liability insurance. However, the total value of the cover provided by the policies must be at least £5 million. You should bear in mind that the £5 million minimum level of cover includes costs, so you may wish to purchase cover of more than this.

When you take out or renew a policy, your insurer will give you a certificate of employers' liability insurance. This must state clearly the minimum level of cover provided and the companies covered by the policy. You must display a copy of the certificate of insurance where your employees can easily read it.

INFORMATION TO EMPLOYEES

Employers must display the approved Health and Safety Law poster required by the Health and Safety, Information to Employees Regulations telling employees what they need to know about health and safety. This is usually displayed on the staff notice board or similar position where all staff can see it.

MEASURING PERFORMANCE

If managing directors or CEOs were asked how they measured their companies' performance, they would probably mention measures like percentage profit, return on investment or market share. A common feature of the measures quoted would be that they are generally positive in nature – reflecting achievement – rather than negative, reflecting failure.

If the same people were asked how they measured their company's health and safety performance, it is likely that the only measure quoted would be injury statistics. While the general business performance of an organisation is subject to a range of positive measures, for health and safety it too often comes down to one negative measure, injury and ill health statistics – measures of failures.

Health and safety performance measurement should seek to answer such questions as:

- Where are we now relative to our overall health and safety aims and objectives?
- Where are we now in controlling hazards and risks?
- How do we compare with others?
- Why are we where we are?
- Are we getting better or worse over time?
- Is our management of health and safety effective (doing the right things)?

- Is our management of health and safety reliable (doing things right consistently)?
- Is our management of health and safety proportionate to our hazards and risks?
- Is our management of health and safety efficient?
- Is an effective health and safety management system in place across all parts of the organisation (deployment)?
- Is our culture supportive of health and safety, particularly in the face of competing demands?

We measure safety performance by monitoring (both proactive and reactive) audits, inspections and reviews.

RISK ASSESSMENT RECORD		
Area:		
Assessment Completed By:		Date:
Activities: (Brief description of the operation)		
Hazards: (What hazards have you found within the work activity? Noise, Manual Handling, Electricity, Fire, Hazardous Substances, Special Effects, Vehicles, Plant and Machinery, Environmental Hazards, Biological Hazards, Slips, Trips, Falls, Stress and Work Hours).		
Number of Persons at Risk: (Approximate Numbers)		
Employees:	Contractors:	Public:

SEVERITY	LIKELIHOOD	RISK CLASS
Equipment Damage No Injury Trivial Injury Minor Injury Major Injury Fatal Injury	Impossible Remote Possible Probable Likely	High Moderate Minor Acceptable

With No Controls:
Worst Likely Outcome: **Likelihood Of Occurrence:**   **Probable Risk Class:**

Current Information:
(What do you know about the hazard, what do the Regulations state and what references or publications have you consulted?)
Codes of Practice
Manufacturers Instructions
Industry Best Practice
HSE Guidance and Regulation
Company Policy and/or Rules
British / European Standards

Current Controls (What controls do you already have in place? Do not state what you intend to do, only what already exists)
Training and Information
Qualification
Supervision
Access Controls/Separation of Traffic
Safety Tests and Inspections
Certification
Structural Calculations
Permits To Work
Safety Rules
Method Statements
Suitable Work Equipment
P.P.E.

ADEQUATE CONTROL: (Are the current controls adequate?)

ACTION PLAN

ACTION REQUIRED: (What are you going to do in terms of removing the hazard or reducing the risk to an acceptable level?)

BY WHOM:

TARGET DATE/TIME: **COMPLETION DATE:**

CONTROLS TO BE MONITORED AND ASSESSED BY:
AND FREQUENCY: (Who is going to monitor the current controls and when / how often?)

A CASE STUDY

A small up-and-coming five piece rock band are undertaking a UK tour in a splitter bus; they (typically) have a very limited budget. The band has two backline technicians, one of which also acts as the stage manager and a tour manager who is also the FOH sound engineer. The tour manager and backline technicians take it in turns to driver the splitter bus. The band is only travelling with guitars, amps/cabs, drum kit, two keyboards and basic spares. They are not carrying lighting of backdrops etc, so there is no work at height required (apart from being on stage). They will headline a number of small gigs during the tour and support a well-known act on other larger dates where they will be required to pay the headline acts monitor engineer and lighting operator to provide services for them. By fully co-operating with venues and promoters and by following the guidance produced in this book the requirements of the CDM Regulations 2015 will have been met by the band.

We will look at the implementation of some of what we have covered so far and all the additional factors and health and safety regulations that cover the work on this tour.

The ultimate employer in this situation will be the artist or the artist management company. They will probably be an organisation or company that employs five or more persons, including employers, directors, partners, etc. as well as all crew members so they must by law produce a written health and safety policy document and risk assessments for the operations to be carried out. A written policy is not required for a company or organisation that employees less than five persons.

Remember, a tour, production manager, crew chief or head of department all have the responsibilities of an employer's representative. For convenience I will refer to these roles as a "line manager" throughout the rest of this book. There is a good possibility you will also be responsible for the selection and management of other staff such as backline technicians.

These responsibilities are yours because of the nature of the work you carry out and not because of your title; you can't discharge your responsibilities simply by changing your title.

Backline technicians have all the responsibilities of a normal self-employed person unless they also employ or supervise other crew.

Line managers have the responsibility of providing information, instruction and supervision as well as assisting with training and helping to ensure the health, safety and welfare of other members of staff.

These responsibilities are not to be taken lightly as they can severely affect the health and safety culture we have been trying to establish. You may breach the law if you do not discharge your duties to the full and this may lead to persecution, fines or even imprisonment. Tour and production managers are responsible for ensuring health and safety legal compliance amongst the whole touring party. Crew chiefs and heads of department have the responsibility of assisting with health and safety compliance within their own section.

The employer will require Public / Employers Liability Insurance – a copy of which should be available to the tour manager to keep on file.

All self-employed persons (freelancers) are required to provide their own Public Liability and if required, Employers Liability Insurance.

The employer or client has a legal responsibility to provide the band and crew with a safe place of work. This will probably be a venue or rehearsal space. The management of the venues they will be working in and the promoters of the shows they are planning also have responsibilities to ensure they have a safe place of work. They may claim not to have any responsibility for their safety but they do!

In turn, the band and crew are contractors working in host venues; they must keep things safe and be professional at all times.

As a tour, stage, production, line manager, head of department or crew chief they must remember they are not Hitler or a policeman. They should offer friendly encouragement and advice to the crew on health and safety matters but they need to be firm where matters of safety are concerned and be prepared to stop any unsafe activity. They are also responsible for the welfare of the crew and enforcing some simple rules such as the correct use of PPE, not allowing alcohol or recreational drugs at work and ensuring the crew get regular good food, have adequate rest breaks and that they are properly hydrated.

The responsibilities of a tour manager or production manager are similar to those of an employer as in effect you will be the employer's representative, but ultimately it is the employer's responsibility to ensure the health, safety and welfare of all employees and freelance contractors as well as providing:

- Instruction
- Information

- Training
- Supervision
- Employers Liability Insurance to cover all employees (but not to contractors or self-employed freelancers).
- PPE (but not to contractors or self-employed freelancers).

But here it can be a little confusing as it is most probable that all crew members are in fact self-employed but fortunately health and safety regulations state you can treat a freelancer as "an employee for health and safety purposes only" without that freelancer losing their self-employed status. Freelancers must still provide their own Public and (if required) Employers Liability Insurance.

WORKING TIME REGULATIONS, TRAVEL AND ACCOMMODATION

Employers have a duty under Section 2 of the Health and Safety at Work Act (HASAWA) to ensure, so far as is reasonably practicable, the health, safety and welfare at work of all their employees. This means they cannot require people to work excessive hours or unsuitable shift patterns likely to lead to ill health or accidents caused by fatigue.

Work schedules should also allow for adequate rest periods. That includes crew driving up and down motorways to attend the endless string of meetings we need to attend as well as crew travelling between gigs. Fatigue increases the risk of accidents and accidents are going to result in reduced productivity.

Under Regulation 3 of the Management of Health and Safety at Work Regulations 1999, employers are required to carry out risk assessment to identify hazards such as fatigue, and evaluate the extent of the risks involved, so that measures can be taken to comply with the general duties under the HASAWA.

The Working Time Regulations don't apply to the genuine self-employed. This is all well and good but the HSE still looks at long working hours as a hazard and will still want risk assessments from self-employed persons working excessive (over eight) hours per day. Just because crew are self-employed does not mean they can (legally) work until they drop – even if the tour manager expects them to do so!

When travelling by trains, boats and planes it is down to the service operators, airports, rail stations and harbours to make the areas safe for passengers. There is no need for you to risk assess these operations; just behave and act like the professionals you should be.

REST BREAKS

Adult employees (over 18 years) are entitled to 11 hours' rest in every 24-hour working period, not less than 24 hours in each 7-day period or 48 hours in each 14-day period.

The employer may decide which of these to apply. Employees are also entitled to 20 minutes' rest after working for six hours. These rest breaks must be uninterrupted.

The Working Time Regulations are very complex and I will not go into them further here.

The role of the tour manager is to first check the distances and time allocated for travel between gigs to ensure there is adequate time for crew to be suitable and adequately rested, recuperated and properly fed between shows so that work and travel can be carried out safely. At no time must drivers or crew exceed allocated working time or tachography regulations; it is not acceptable to set off late at night after a gig in a splitter bus driven by tired crew members just to enable the touring party to reach the next gig by load in time. That situation is an accident just waiting to happen and safety is always your first priority so you must investigate alternative travel such as a sleeper bus, rescheduling or even cancelling a show if you think there is a possibility of not getting adequate rest and recuperation or have tried crew acting as drivers.

ACCOMMODATION

It's worth investing in the most comfortable forms of travel and accommodation as possible while on the road as long uncomfortable journeys, poor food, poor accommodation and poor service will almost invariably lead to tiredness, rows, arguments, stress and poor moral. In the UK we have some control as the tour manager (often aided by a music industry travel agent) will almost certainly be booking the hotels but in Europe hotels will normally be provided by the promoter so we have far less control over quality of hotels and it is common to find that your hotel has been down-graded at the last minute because ticket sales are not as good as originally predicted by the promoter.

TRAVEL INSURANCE AND FIRST AID

The Employer should provide good quality insurance for employees. Self-employed freelancers should provide their own Medical and Repatriation Insurance and it is prudent to insure items such as bank cards and other items of value. Make sure this is from a good quality insurer and covers all your requirements; there are a lot of Insurance Policies that are cheap and provide very limited cover.

Employers are also responsible of ensuring that first aid facilities (including first aiders) are provided to all employees. This responsibility cannot be transferred to the promoter or venue even by contract or rider, self-employed freelancers should provide their own simple first aid kit that is suitable for treating them-selves at work. A touring party should carry a first aid kit and have properly qualified first aiders among the crew so the whole party has access to the facilities. The tour/production manager should arrange this and get all parties to sign an agreement form to say they accept this arrangement.

The tour or production manager should carry out an assessment of first aid needs and implement the outcomes.

Your risk assessment will almost certainly show that you will require one emergency first aider and a first aid kit suitable to treat up to ten persons; these can be purchased from a decent pharmacy for only a few pounds. Any use of equipment must be reported so it can be restocked.

ACCIDENT AND INCIDENT REPORTING

The tour or production manager should ensure that **ALL** accidents and incidents however minor they may seem (including near misses) are recoded in the Accident Book (ISBN: 9780717664580). These are available for only a couple of pounds from HSE Books (https://books.hse.gov.uk) and are again essential items to be carried along with the first aid kit. The Accident Book contains simple information on what and how to make reports.

Anyone making a report that did not witness the incident should only state what they actually saw or were told by the person involved. For instance if a work mate tells them that they fell off a chair when changing a light bulb but they did not see him or her fall you will report as follows: "Fred *said* he fell off a chair when changing a light bulb". Do not speculate in your report as to what may have happened.

You may be requested to complete the accident books for the promoter, the venue and any service companies that may have been involved in the incident. This is quite normal practice.

All accidents and near misses must be investigated. The objective will always be to establish how the accident happened so systems and controls can be put in place to prevent reoccurrence and not to apportion blame. Crew should have no fear in reporting accidents, they are not going to get in trouble.

RIDDOR (Reporting of Injuries, Diseases and Dangerous Occurrences Regulations 2013), requires employers to report certain work-related accidents, diseases and dangerous occurrences to the authorities. It applies to all work activities, but not to all incidents.

Reporting accidents and ill health at work is a legal requirement. The information enables the enforcing authorities to identify where and how risks arise and to investigate serious accidents.

You will need to report:

- Deaths
- Major injuries
- Accidents resulting in over seven day injury
- Diseases
- Dangerous occurrences

Major Injuries include:

- fractures, other than to the fingers, thumbs or toes
- amputations
- any injury likely to lead to permanent loss of sight or reduction in sight
- any crush injury to the head or torso causing damage to the brain or internal organs
- serious burns (including scalding) which:
  - covers more than 10% of the body
  - causes significant damage to the eyes, respiratory system or other vital organs
- any scalping requiring hospital treatment
- any loss of consciousness caused by head injury or asphyxia
- any other injury arising from working in an enclosed space which:

- leads to hypothermia or heat-induced illness
- requires resuscitation or admittance to hospital for more than 24 hours

If there is an accident connected with work (including an act of physical violence) and an employee (including a self-employed person) suffers an over-seven-day injury then it must report it to the enforcing authority within fifteen days.

An over-seven-day injury is one which is not "major" but results in the injured person being away from work or unable to do the full range of their normal duties for more than seven days. The day of the accident is not counted towards making up the seven days but weekends and rest days DO count.

If a doctor notifies you that your employee suffers from a reportable work-related disease then you must report it to the enforcing authority.

Reportable diseases include:

- carpal tunnel syndrome;
- severe cramp of the hand or forearm;
- occupational dermatitis;
- hand-arm vibration syndrome;
- occupational asthma;
- tendonitis or tenosynovitis of the hand or forearm;
- any occupational cancer;
- any disease attributed to an occupational exposure to a biological agent.

If something happens which does not result in a reportable injury, but which clearly could have done, then it may be a dangerous occurrence which must be reported immediately.

Dangerous Occurrences include:

- the collapse, overturning or failure of load-bearing parts of lifts and lifting equipment;
- plant or equipment coming into contact with overhead power lines;
- the accidental release of any substance which could cause injury to any person.

All accidents, diseases and dangerous occurrences should be reported to the Incident Contact Centre. The Contact Centre was established as a single point of contact for receiving all incidents in the UK.

You can report incidents by any of the following routes:
- Telephone – 0845 3009923
- Internet – Reports can be made using the online reporting system (www.hse.riddor.gov.uk)

The Incident Contact Centre will forward details of incidents to the relevant enforcing authority.

Records of any reportable injury, disease or dangerous occurrence must be kept.

These must include:
- The date and method of reporting
- The date, time and place of the event
- Personal details of those involved
- A brief description of the nature of the event or disease.

EQUIPMENT

Check all equipment carefully when packing to ensure all equipment is safe and that all electrical equipment has been portable appliance tested (PAT). The tour or production manager should hold copies of all the certificates. Don't forget spares such as white gaffer tape and RCDs. Make sure your flight cases are also in good order and that the wheels operate smoothly.

Any fabrics such as backdrops must have a current Fire Test Certificate. The tour or production manager should again hold copies of these.

Never leave flight cases open, a heavy lid dropping can easily sever cables or fingers and butterfly catches snag on clothing and skin leaving nasty scratches and cuts.

Carefully planning your equipment needs is essential to the safe and smooth running of a tour.

DRIVING

Obviously drivers of self-drive hire vehicles must be in possession of a valid driving licence for the type of vehicle involved and hold the correct insurance cover. This will normally be provided by the hire company but I must mention insurance for self-drive "splitter buses" has insurance for these vehicles can be a minefield. Most hire companies will require drivers to be over 25 years old; if you hold the new style photo driving licence then you will require the photo card and the paper counterpart.

You will need "Category B" which is a normal car licence. "Category B" is a vehicle less than 3500kg (3.5 tonnes) with no more than eight passenger seats not including the driver's seat – so nine in total. This can be identified on the rear of your licence.

- "Category C" covers any vehicle over 3500kg (3.5 tonnes)
- "Category D" covers any vehicle with more than nine seats including the driver i.e. ten and 11 seat vehicles.

Please note regardless of the above you cannot charge people to drive them around without correct 'hire and reward' licence and insurance.

The DVLA has a website explaining all licences: http://www.direct.gov.uk/en/Motoring/DriverLicensing/WhatCanYouDriveAndYourObligations/index.htm.

The tour manager should remind drivers to carry out daily safety checks on all vehicles including;

- Lights
- Horn
- Tyres
- Fluids (Fuel, Oil, Coolant and Washer Fluid)
- Breaks
- Washers and Wipers

When hiring a vehicle please ensure it comes with:

- Full UK/EU breakdown assistance
- Spare wheel, jack, etc.
- Fire extinguisher and first aid kit.
- All necessary documentation including hire documents, insurance, tax and copy of the MOT test certificate.

Persons using their own vehicles for work purposes must ensure they have insurance to cover business related travel and not just social, domestic and pleasure. Business travel can include going to the bank or post office, travelling from job to job, transporting colleagues or tools and equipment etc. Tour and production managers should make the required checks.

Finally, plan your route carefully. Google Maps and Sat Navs are wonderful for this. Ensure you are properly equipped, check weather conditions before setting off and allow plenty of time for the journey including rest breaks. A simple travel risk assessment should be completed, implemented and filed.

Tune your radio in to receive traffic and weather news. Drive safely!

At the venue, find a sensible place to park as close to the stage/access door as possible. At a festival you will probably be instructed where to park. Follow these instructions carefully and do not block access routes or fire lanes or you may find your vehicle being towed away. Festival sites usually have strict speed limits. Ensure you follow them and any specific directions you may be given.

Do not under any circumstances drive on a festival, event or venue site with hazard lights on as this prevents others seeing when you are indicating and conflicts with the Road Traffic Act that states hazard lights are to be only used on stationary vehicles. Use an orange warning beacon if you have one or dipped head lights.

When parking at a hotel or overnight, try and back the vehicle tight up to a wall. This will help prevent thieves from gaining access to the rear doors.

Ensure that all equipment and baggage is stowed correctly in splitter buses and sleeper buses. A laptop computer falling from a luggage rack can do a lot of damage to a person's head! Don't forget to remind fellow passengers to be careful when getting off a tour bus or splitter; they may be stepping into a traffic lane. A number of nasty accidents have happened when crew members have stepped off a bus in a service station.

INDUCTIONS

You may have to undergo a safety induction before being allowed into a festive, venue or event site. Take part in this induction willingly and happily; it's for the safety of everyone. If an induction is not given then tour or production managers should obtain the required information and provide the induction at each and every venue before the 'load-in' or any other work starts. All crew should be present for this briefing that should only take a few minutes. An induction check list is included at the back of this book.

Inductions are an important part of the safety management process and everyone has a duty to take part in this procedure.

At no time block or prop open fire doors and do not cover or obscure anything provided in the interests of safety. That includes safety signs and fire fighting equipment.

LOADING /UNLOADING VEHICLES AND MANUAL HANDLING

Parking and unloading/loading on the road outside a venue can be very hazardous. Ensure you have a safe working area to unload your vehicle. The venue may be able to assist with warning cones or temporary barriers. At a festival you can probable back right up to the stage loading bay.

Check the route into the venue is clear and all doors are open; be extremely careful to protect pedestrians outside the venue when loading in your equipment. Wear high visibility tabards and safety footwear. When opening van or truck doors, be vigilant in case equipment and cases have become unstable in transit. Use the van or truck door as a shield when first opening doors in case items drop. Keep others at a safe distance. People have been killed when this has happened in the past and a Risk Assessment is required for the operation. Finally, check you have adequate work lights on the route as it will probably be dark when you load out after the show and adequate lighting is essential to safety.

LOCAL CREW

Local crew provided by the promoter or venue can vary considerably. Some turn up on time looking smart and ready for work in the crewing company's shirt so they can easily be identified. Some are late and look like they have not slept for days, lack personal hygiene standards and have a bad attitude. Check they have protective footwear, high visibility tabards and gloves. Do not allow these who are not properly equipped to work; you should be able to charge the promoter the fee that would normally be paid to any of the local crew that are unusable.

The experience and knowledge of local crew can also vary considerably. Some know all about back line and how to set it up correctly, some don't have a clue. It's safest to assume they know nothing.

Self-employed (freelance) operators who either instruct or supervise other crew take on responsibility for the way their crew operates and in effect becomes their employer. If one of the crew you are supervising or instructing suffers an injury, it is then possible for them to sue you for damages even though you do not pay or employ them. Tour, stage, production managers and crew chiefs, etc. should make a special note of this advice. With the Employers Liability Cover, you will have legal representation for your defence and payment of damages, if they are awarded against you. Employers Liability Insurance may be a useful consideration and can be purchased as a package with your Public Liability Insurance.

MANUAL HANDLING

The manual handling regulations were covered in the first book of this trilogy, *Health and Safety in the Live Music And Event Technical Production Industry*, so I do not intend to repeat that information again here but tour and production managers should ensure they and their crew have received manual handling training and use any required PPE such as safety footwear and gloves. Please also ensure local crew have also received manual handling training and are equipped with safety footwear and gloves. It's a good idea to make this a condition in the technical rider.

If your flightcases are not all fitted with wheels it's a good idea to carry a simple wheel dolly to aid in moving your equipment safely and easily.

In some situations small acts will have to load their own equipment in and out of the venue and as we have previously seen, the Health and Safety at Work Act requires everyone to protect themselves while at work so when musicians are moving their own equipment they have no excuse for not wearing PPE such as protective footwear. They may not be very happy about this and the Tour Manager may be the most unpopular person in the world if he insists upon this but it's something that has to be worked out and a musician with a broken foot may jeopardise all the forthcoming gigs that are booked.

STAGES AND RISERS

Take a look at the stage or platform you are supposed to work on. Some shoddy clubs have very poor quality stages. Run up and down ramps and steps to make sure they and safe and secure. Stages should have hand/kick rails or walls on three sides as well as on steps and ramps. The platform itself should not bounce up and down when you walk across it. Checks are simple but essential. The downstage edge of the stage, risers and steps should be marked with a 50mm wide white strip, if no strips are present use white gaffer tape. People have fallen off stages and risers that have not been marked and have then successfully sued those in control. You have to protect your band and crew. It's a good idea to use empty flightcases, etc. then build a temporary barrier across the downstage edge of the stage during load in and load out to prevent anyone falling off the stage.

The band's stage drinks should be limited to what is absolutely necessary and no more to avoid spillages. Small bottles of water with sports caps are ideal. Place them on a tray of rack case cover in case of spills. The best position for them is on the front of the drum.

Low lighting levels make stages very hazardous. Ensure you have a trusty Mag-Lite or head set touch available to you. I'm sure you know it's particularly useful for getting the band on and off stage.

ELECTRICS

Checking your equipment before any tour is vital: 95% of all faults can be found in the visual inspection that is part of the portable appliance test (PAT). Some venues will not allow untested equipment on their premises. Get all you equipment, leads and cables inspected and tested.

Good cable management is the sign of a true professional operation. Keep all your leads neat and tidy, use matting and gaffer tape to cover, protect and secure your leads and cables, prevent trip hazards on stage.

Remind the backline technicians to use RCDs for added protection.

If you're unsure of the power supply it may be useful to have a piece of test equipment to check phasing. These are commonly known as Martindales. As a rule of thumb guide, in the UK power supplies are generally safe but the further you travel from the UK the more you need to check. If it looks unsafe, it probably is unsafe!

WORK AT HEIGHT

You should have no valid reason for working at height, unless your crew trained and equipped to do so you should not do any work at height and that includes step ladders. Use the house riggers to rig and focus lamps as well as hanging you back drop, unless you can lower bars or trusses to rig this yourself at ground level.

Technically you are working at height unless the down stage edge of the stage is barricaded. You can use flightcases to build a temporary barrier while you work on stage.

NOISE

It's almost 100% certain that you, your crew and the band will be working in areas where the volume of sound will be above 85dB for long periods of time and this can soon cause irreparable damage to your hearing. A hearing aid will not help you once your hearing is damaged: hearing damage is different to being deaf.

Remind you crew of this fact and ensure they use ear protection when the volume is above 85dB; it is a legal requirement under the Noise at Work Regulations. As a rule of thumb guide, if you can't hear somebody talking to you in a normal voice when they are two metres from you then the background noise is above 85dB.

Ensure you carry a good supply of disposable hearing protectors on tour and use them. Generally speaking, ear plugs provide better protection than ear muffs, they are very cheap and are to be recommended.

Give your crew and band a five minute lesson on how to fit and use ear plugs, they will benefit from this. Giving this instruction, training and information is all part of your legal duties.

Disposable Ear Plug Fitting Instructions

Before fitting any ear plugs, make sure your hands are clean.

Hold the ear plug between your thumb and forefinger. Roll and compress the entire ear plug to a small, crease-free cylinder.	1. Roll entire earplug into a crease-free cylinder 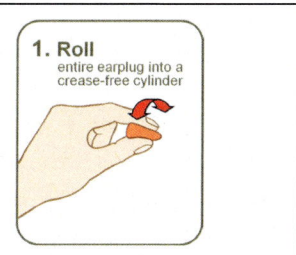

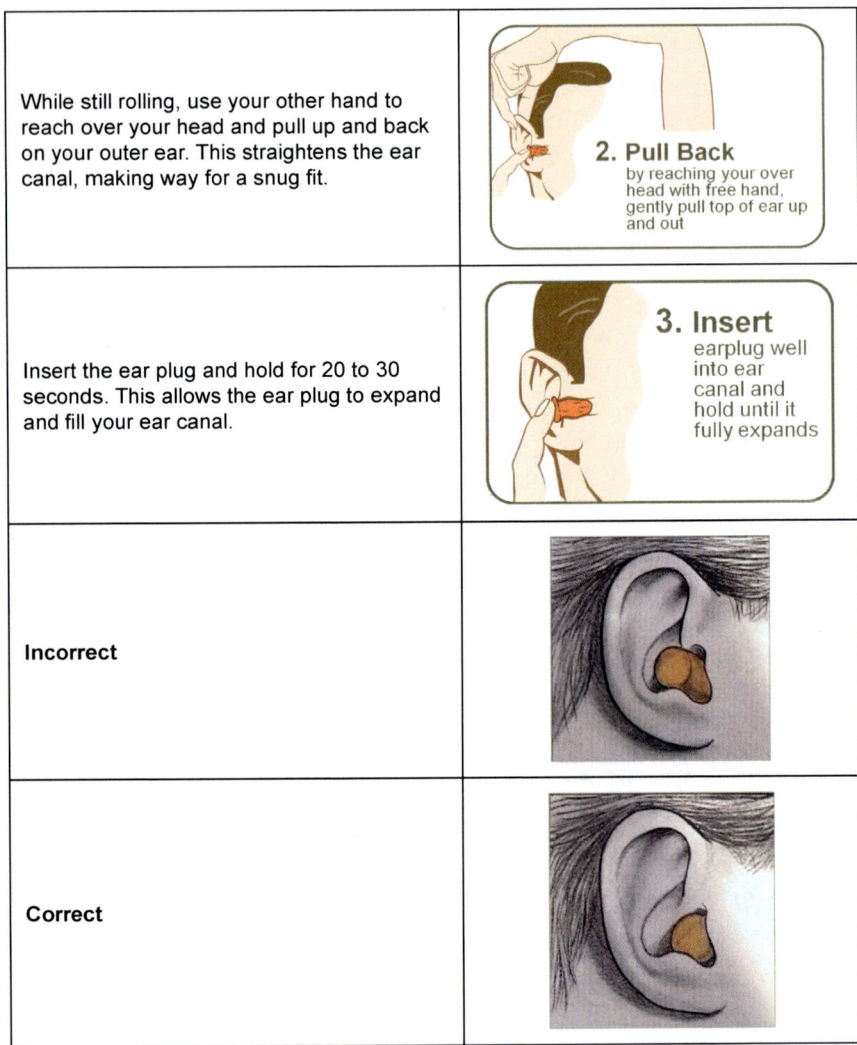

While still rolling, use your other hand to reach over your head and pull up and back on your outer ear. This straightens the ear canal, making way for a snug fit.	**2. Pull Back** by reaching your over head with free hand, gently pull top of ear up and out
Insert the ear plug and hold for 20 to 30 seconds. This allows the ear plug to expand and fill your ear canal.	**3. Insert** earplug well into ear canal and hold until it fully expands
Incorrect	
Correct	

SPECIAL EFFECTS

Each of these effects can make the subject of an ideal "Tool Box Talk". Stage, tour or production managers should ensure these procedures are followed. Only the most common and basic effects are listed here.

Strobes

Strobe lighting can induce epilepsy in some extreme cases so to reduce the risk strobes must be operated in accordance with the guidance set out in the *Purple Guide*.

When strobe lights are used at venues, flicker rates should be kept at or below four flashes per second.

Below this rate it is estimated that only 5% of the flicker-sensitive population will be at risk of an attack. This flicker rate only applies to the overall output of any group of lights in direct view, but where more than one strobe light is used the flashes should be synchronised.

Everyone must be informed if strobes are to be used and warning signs must be erected if necessary.

Ultraviolet light

Powerful ultraviolet light can sensitise exposed areas of the skin in very rare cases. If any member of staff experiences skin sensitisation they should remove themselves from the area of the ultraviolet light and seek medical aid.

Ultraviolet lighting must be rigged at a minimum of 16ft. away from any person who may come into contact with it during use and only used when following manufacturers instructions and with a very high standard of safety and maintenance.

Ensure that lamps are used correctly to restrict exposure to ultraviolet radiation and in particular to UVB radiation.

To remove UVB radiation, some lamps have a double skin whereas other manufacturers provide lamp housings, which have separate filters. Lamps should not be used if the outer skin is broken or if the housing filter is not in place.

Lasers

Lasers come into a special category. Do not touch or tamper with laser equipment and do not look straight into the beam of the laser to avoid possible damage to eyes. Keep at a safe distance to avoid burns.

Lamps and HMI Lamp Systems

Gauntlets covering wrist arteries, and a full face visor covering neck arteries should be worn while handing the lamps. Xenon and HMI lamps of 5kW and 7kW are pressurised to about eight bar when cold and around 30 bar when hot and so a lamp burst is possible with the resultant danger from flying glass. When the lamp is being installed, people should vacate the vicinity until the projector housing is closed. It is not advisable to carry out this operation with the audience present.

The arc of xenon and HMI lamps are very bright and housings are designed so that the arc cannot be viewed directly by the operator.

Care should be taken that people are not put at risk by 'blinding' them with the light, especially if they are moving around in otherwise dark environments (e.g. while entering or leaving a venue).

Other Lighting Effects

One addition to this list is Sharpys. No, not the pen but a lighting fixture with a narrow, sharp and intense beam that focuses outside of the lamp unit, rather like a magnifying glass. If you place your hand in the beam close to the lamp it will not appear hot but further away and you can rapidly burn your hand and this heat can burn items such as drapes and softs as well as span sets so they have the potential of being very dangerous. Even the lamp housing gets very hot so care must be exercised when placing the lamps away from drapes, especially if fans are in use for smoke and haze effects that may blow drapes dangerously close to lighting fixtures. The manufacturers have engraved a warning onto the body of the fixture to ensure users rig these lights at a safe distance from objects that may burn or melt and this advice must be followed strictly unless you want to melt your stage set and rigging or start a fire. I am aware of one tour where a choir was almost reduced to a crisp on stage by these lights!

Smoke, Vapour and Fog Effects

Employees must follow the same basic safety rules that apply to all types of smoke machine:

- The machine must be in a fixed position and adequately protected from interference. Some machines can get very hot during use.
- A competent operator should be with the machine.
- All machines must be used in accordance with the manufacturer's instructions

- Fans may be used to direct the smoke or vapour but care must be taken to prevent the spread of smoke or vapour into public areas. This may cause an audience to panic.
- Smoke and vapour must not be discharged or allowed to drift into exits, stairways, escape routes, or be allowed to obscure exit signs or fire protection equipment. Some fluids, cracked oil in particular, leave a deposit on stage which can prove a dangerous slip hazard.

If fire or smoke detection equipment is fitted within a venue special care must be taken. Some venues and Entertainment Licence conditions do not allow the use of smoke or fog machines because of these detectors.

If they are in use the amount of smoke or fog must be restricted to prevent these detectors operating. On no account must employees try to prevent smoke detectors operating by covering them, over riding or switching them off.

Some smoke fluids are known to cause discomfort to those who suffer from smoke allergy or asthma. Avoid the use of such fluids where possible.

Show Stop Procedure

Stopping a show is a real emergency last resort. Nobody wants to do it but sometimes it is essential and when that time comes everyone must act in the correct manner and like a well-oiled machine. The type of emergencies that will require a show to be stopped include fire, bomb threat or similar need to evacuate the venue, or it could be a crowd management situation where people are getting crushed, injured or asphyxiated. In these situations you only have a few minutes to act to enable lives to be saved.

Again, advance planning is essential. A designated member of the crew that the band know and respect should go on stage and stop the band and get the sound engineer to cut the volume. A prepared message informing and instructing the audience is then read out. Lighting should be set to plain static white light and house lights switched on.

It may be that the show only needs to stop for a few minutes before it can safely be resumed.

Every situation is different but full cooperation must be given by everyone in a Show Stop situation.

Miscellaneous Hazards

Some artists have the terrible habit of throwing items into the audience from the stage (including themselves) such as drum sticks, items of clothing, etc. This habit should be strongly discouraged as a drum stick sticking into somebody's eye is not at all pleasant and may lead to criminal prosecution; at least one musician I know of was prosecuted for injuring an audience member after they were hit by a guitar he hurled into the audience. If nobody is injured a crowd serge caused by audience trying to grasp the thrown object as a souvenir can also cause major problems that can lead to fatalities.

Stage diving by performers is also a no-no. At least one performer has been severely injured when the audience failed to catch them and at least one has ended up in hospital when they fell from stage structures and rigging that failed to support them. It's lucky no audience members have not been severely injured by such stupid antics.

A great many problems can be prevented by not having guests on stage (including agents, managers, press, etc.) in dangerous working areas so exclude them from the outset. A stage is supposed to be your safe working area.

An example of the kind of checks that should be carried out is shown here:

Ensure crew report for work in a fit condition, properly equipped and not under the effects of drink or drugs. Ensure crew get adequate rest, meal and refreshment breaks during the working day.
Ensure all crew have been given an induction at each new venue.
Check all edges of stages, steps and ramps are marked with a strip white tape or paint. During build and breakdown, arrange for the edge of stage to be taped and fenced or barriered off.
Check that fire extinguishers are placed on stage and ensure that at no time these are covered or obscured. If any extinguisher is used at any time it's use must be reported so that it can be replaced or refilled without delay. Water extinguishers must not be placed on stage. Only CO_2 or Dry Powder extinguishers must be placed near electrical equipment.

Keep the stage as clean and tidy as possible. Brooms, bin bags and bins must be available. Designate a crew member to keep the area (including below stage) free of combustible materials.
Confine drinks and liquids to one safe area of the sage away from electrical items. Other than essential crew and performance drinks all other drinks and liquids are banned from directly on stage. Persons with stage access can assist by not bringing drinks onto the stage. Half full bottles, cans and glasses are a real problem as well as a hazard.
Before equipment changeovers, all cans, bottles and glasses should be removed from the stage by an appointed crew member.
Stage access is only granted to performers, production and "house" crew. Assist with keeping all unauthorised persons off the stage, this includes press, photographers, record company staff, agents, artists friends, family and managers, etc. Stewards backstage will also assist with the task if requested.
Ensure adequate work lights are in position for night work and "load out".
Press, guests and photographers must not be sent to the FOH Mix or Pit Area, they are not viewing areas.
The stage and area around it will be a Noise Protection Zone. Tour and Production Managers are required to assist with enforcement of the Noise at Work Regulations by insisting that crew and other persons entering the Noise Protection Zones use ear protection.
Ensure that crew (including Local Crew) and all other persons use all required Personal Protective Equipment (including safety footwear when involved in manual handling operations). No boots – no job!
Ensure that flight cases (including empty cases) are stacked or stored in a safe manner that does not block or obscure fire exits, emergency routes or fire fighting equipment.
Ensure that all performers and crew are aware of special effects including strobes, lasers, UV, smoke and vapour. Everyone (including pit teams) must know the position of pyrotechnics and the times they are to be operated.
UV lighting must be rigged at least 16ft. from crew and performers. Ensure warning notices are in position if UV and strobes are in use.
Ensure a competent person is positioned by any smoke and vapour effect machines at all times during use.
All leads and cables must be covered or laid in such a way as not to be a hazard.
Establish "Safe Working Areas".

General Safety Rules

1. All employees should be aware of, respect and adhere to the rules and procedures contained in the Health and Safety policy.
2. All employees shall immediately report any unsafe practices or conditions to the relevant authority.
3. Any person under the influence of alcohol or any other intoxicating drug, which might impair motor skills or judgement, whether prescribed or otherwise, shall not be allowed to work.
4. Horseplay, practical joking or any other acts, which might jeopardise the health and safety of any other persons, are forbidden.
5. Any person whose levels of alertness and / or ability are reduced due to illness or fatigue will not be allowed to work if this might jeopardise the health and safety of that person or any other person.
6. Employees shall not adjust, move or otherwise tamper with any electrical equipment or machinery in a manner not within the scope of their duties, unless instructed to do so by a senior member of staff.
7. All waste materials must be disposed of carefully and in such a way that they do not constitute a hazard to other workers.
8. No worker should undertake a job which appears to be unsafe.
9. No worker should undertake a job until he or she has received adequate safety instruction and is authorised to carry out the task.
10. All injuries must be reported to the delegated representative.
11. Employees should take care to ensure that all protective guards and other safety devices are properly fitted and in good working order and shall immediately report any deficiencies to the supervisor.
12. Work shall be well planned and supervised to avoid injuries in the handling of heavy materials and while using equipment.
13. No employees should use chemicals without the knowledge required to work with those chemicals safely.
14. Suitable clothing and footwear will be worn at all times. Personal protective equipment shall be worn wherever appropriate.
15. All employees are expected to attend safety meetings if required.
16. The use of alcohol and recreational drugs is strictly prohibited. Any employee found to be consuming or under the influence of alcohol or recreational drugs IS LIABLE TO INSTANT DISMISSAL.

Working Environment

1. The working environment must be kept clean and tidy.
2. Any spillages must be cleaned up immediately according to appropriate procedures.
3. Waste materials and rubbish must be routinely removed and placed into bins or skips for disposal.
4. All open pits, trenches, holes, etc must be covered when not in use and clearly marked using the appropriate warning signs.
5. Leads and cables must be laid and suitable covered in a way so as not to prevent hazard.
6. Chemical waste must not be discarded into sinks, toilets, streams or other water courses.
7. Aerosols and chemical containers must be discarded according to the appropriate procedures, not into fires.
8. Employees are advised to always wash their hands before eating and drinking.

Walkways, Steps and Stages

1. Walkways, passageways steps and stages must be kept clear from obstructions at all times.
2. If a walkway, passageway, steps or stage becomes wet it should be clearly marked with warning signs and/or covered with non-slip material
3. Trailing cables are a trip hazard and should not be left in any walk or passageway.
4. The down stage edge of all stages, treads and platforms must be clearly marked with white gaffer tape.
5. In areas of low lighting (stage and backstage areas) any change in the floor elevation of any walkway or passageway must be clearly marked (white gaffer tape).
6. Where objects are stored in or around a passageway, care must be taken to ensure that no long or sharp edges jut out into the passageway or walkway in such a way as to constitute a safety hazard.
7. Where a passageway is being used by any vehicles or other moving machinery an alternative route should be used by pedestrians wherever possible. If no alternative route is possible the area should be clearly

marked with warning signs and any additional precautions as may be required must be taken to ensure safety.

Tool and Equipment Maintenance

1. Company vehicles, machinery and tools are only to be used by qualified and authorised personnel. It is the responsibility of the supervisor to determine who is authorised to use specific tools, vehicles and equipment.
2. It is the responsibility of all employees to ensure that any tools, vehicles or equipment they use are in a good and safe condition.
3. Any broken, damaged or faulty work equipment (including electrical equipment) must be clearly marked to indicate that it is non serviceable, taken out of service and reported to management so that it can be replaced or repaired.
4. All tools and equipment must be properly and safely stored when not in use.
5. No tool should be used without the manufacturer's recommended shields, guards or attachments.
6. Approved personal protective equipment must be properly used where appropriate.
7. Persons using machine tools must not wear clothing, jewellery, laminate passes, wrist bands or long hair in such a way as might pose a risk to their or anyone else's safety.
8. Employees are prohibited from using any tool, vehicles or piece of equipment for any purpose other than its intended purpose.

Personal Protective Equipment

1. Employees must use all personal protective equipment provided to them in accordance with the training and instruction given to them regarding its use.
2. Employees who have been provided with personal protective equipment must immediately report any loss of, damage or obvious defect in any equipment provided to their supervisor or the safety director.
3. Gloves should always be used when handling litter, waste and chemicals of any kind. Eye protection should also be used when handling chemicals.

Manual Handling, Lifting and Moving

1. Lifting and moving of objects should always be done by mechanical devices rather than manual handling wherever reasonably practicable. The equipment used should be appropriate for the task at hand.
2. The load to be lifted or moved must be inspected for sharp edges, slivers and wet or greasy patches.
3. When lifting or moving a load with sharp or splintered edges gloves must be worn. Gloves should be free from oil, grease or other agents, which might impair grip.
4. Protective footwear must be used when lifting any heavy load or a load that is capable of damaging the feet if dropped.
5. The route over which the load is to be lifted or moved should be inspected to ensure that it is free of obstructions or spillage which could cause tripping or spillage.
6. Employees should not attempt to lift or move a load, which is too heavy to manage comfortably.
7. Where team lifting or moving is necessary one person should act as co-ordinator, giving commands to lift, lower, etc.
8. Trucks to be loaded or unloaded must be parked on a firm level surface with the engine off and the hand-break on. Staff should stand well clear until the driver has opened the truck doors, just in case the load has shifted during transit or there are loose objects at the rear of the pack that may fall when the doors are opened. Only authorised company personnel shall undertake the loading or unloading of trucks.
9. When unloading or loading vehicles in the street a "safe working area" must be established using cones, bollards and safety barriers.
10. When lifting an object off the ground employees should assume a squatting position, keeping the back straight. The load should be lifted by straightening the knees, not the back. These steps should be reversed for lowering an object to the ground.
11. When carrying bin bags, half fill them and carry them away from your body to avoid cuts and jabs; the bag may contain broken glass or other sharp objects. Always use gloves when handling litter and waste and wash your hands after work.

Electrical Safety

1. Electrical work must only be carried out by competent and qualified persons.
2. Portable power tools for use outdoors must be of the 110 Volt (CET) type.
3. All electrical equipment owned and supplied by the Company will receive regular portable appliance testing (PAT). Employees shall not use their own electrical equipment unless it has been PAT tested and permission obtained from the management.
4. All electrical equipment must be given a visual inspection by the operator before use. This should include checking the plug for damage or burn/scorch marks, inspecting the lead for damage, checking that all connections are secure and that the equipment is in a good state or repair.
5. All electrical equipment must be used with a fuse of the correct rating.
6. If a piece of equipment keeps "tripping out" (more than two or three times) an RCD or MCB, then that equipment should not be used until it has been checked and tested by a competent person and any fault corrected. Apart from checking that a fuse of the correct rating is fitted there is little more a non-qualified person can do. Never try to remove or short circuit the trip, it is almost certainly your appliance that is at fault.
    Note: An MCB (overload trip) is far less sensitive than an RCD (earth leakage trip). An appliance well within the rating of an MCB may well trip out if it has a fault when connected to a system with an RCD.
7. The fault may not have shown up before if is had been used on a non-RCD system, such as domestic installation that is not normally fitted with RCD protection.
8. Any coiled mains lead will heat up in use. To prevent this, extension leads or reels should be fully unwound from their drums before use or they may heat up, melt together and cause a fire.
9. Multi-way adapters (two or three way blocks) that allow more than one appliance to be run from one socket are a major danger. The rule is one appliance to one socket.
10. Employees should report all faults and damage immediately and that piece of equipment taken out of service until it has been repaired. Employees must be on the lookout for possible dangers such as damaged/faulty plugs and equipment, frayed cable, loose connections and poorly laid cables.

11. Checks must be made to see all connections are safe and tamper proof.
12. All electrical connections must be made with the correct connectors and the correct gauges of cable. If in doubt, ask!
13. Never turn on the power to any equipment unless you have checked that it is safe to do so.
14. Employees must not touch or tamper with such connections unless they are qualified or have been given clear instruction about connecting and disconnecting and they are certain that the system is "dead" and therefore safe.

All crew should remember the phrase: See it – sort it! *It is your problem.*

So thank you for reading so far, you now should have enough information to safely tackle basic touring. The final book in this trilogy covers the next level up: festivals, stadium, and arena shows, touring and working with full production and all the hazards that come with that such as plant, work at height, special effects, power, structures, rigging and many other assorted hazards.

SELF-EMPLOYMENT IN THE LIVE MUSIC AND EVENTS INDUSTRY

A Guide for the Self-Employed and those who use the services of the Self-Employed

DISCLAIMER

This document is presented in good faith as guidance only but every assurance is given that it has been checked by a chartered accountant, a solicitor, a tax inspector and an insurance broker. The author cannot be held responsible for any omissions or errors, nor for any consequences arising from acting or not acting on the information given. You are advised to contact your tax or legal advisor, local tax office or insurance broker if you are unsure or have any queries.

Self-Employment vs PAYE – Words of warning
Chris Hannam and Nick Cook

"The tax rules for self-employed people are designed to reflect the day-to-day transactions of the true risk-taking entrepreneur. Genuine self-employment is about being in business on one's own account and not simply applying a label of self-employment." – HMCR

With the introduction of self-assessment in 1997 HMCR gained the power to mount an investigation into any company or individual, at random and without giving any reason or warning. At the end of 2001 a small set and decoration company in Berkshire was subject to just such an investigation. HMCR decided that the freelancers they had been using were booked under terms and conditions which meant they were classed as employees rather than self-employed subcontractors. As is usual in these cases the Revenue said that the money paid to these freelancers over the last few years was just their net pay. The arrears bill sent the company into liquidation. Some while earlier a generator and power distribution supplier to the event industry found itself landed with an arrears bill of around £70,000 for National Insurance Contributions, again because its freelancers were booked in a way that made them employees of the company, rather than self-employed subcontractors. More recently it has been reported that a number of artists have also been under investigation and ordered to pay tax on the backline technicians they engaged as they were deemed by HMCR to be employees and not self-employed.

While these cases alone do not amount to a campaign against the Industry by HMCR, they may well be the shape of things to come. Our industry is a sitting duck for this kind of attention from the tax man because most freelancers are either operating in a way or being booked in a manner that prevents them from being classed as genuinely self-employed. The fundamental problem is that both freelancers and their clients want to enjoy all the financial benefits of self-employment, but either refuse to accept, or are unaware of, the responsibilities that go with that particularly special status. There is a common, even wilful, misconception on all sides of the industry that "freelance automatically equals self-employed", which is simply not the case.

A 'freelancer' is merely someone who supplies services to a number of different clients. They can be taxed for each job either under Schedule D or PAYE, depending on how they operate their 'business' and the terms under which their services are engaged; NOT according to what the freelancer or their accountant may think. A 'freelancer' (or rather 'contractor') may be taxed as self- employed for one job, but under PAYE for the next, even if supplying services to the same client, according to the terms and conditions under which their services have been engaged on each job.

Freelancers and those who use them must stop thinking of freelancers as though they were 'temporary employees' and must start treating them as 'contractors', their correct status if they are to be classed as genuinely self-employed.

The HMCR website is a mine of information on this subject. Clear cut explanations of the regulations regarding employed vs self-employed and what they mean to us all, in frighteningly plain English, can be found there.

Of particular relevance to our industry are the IR 35 and IR 56 Regulations, which basically determine under what conditions a person may be deemed truly self-employed.

While it's true these days that many companies insist on their crews having their own insurance, tools and safety kit, not all of them do.

Even when they do, a lot of them blow it immediately by sending out purchase orders booking people for x days at y pounds per day with z per diems; conditions which, in the eyes of a tax inspector, define their subcontractors as PAYE-taxable employees. What (very basically) should happen here is that a purchase order should only show the total price for the job 'as quoted' by the subcontractor for 'providing services as...' Even then, would a tax man really believe that this group of 'self-employed subcontractors' had 'just happened' to quote exactly the same price as each other on every single job? It was actually the notion of the daily rate that did for the set company mentioned at the start of this section. Even so, we still continue to meet far too many 'subcontractors' who not only don't have, but are still completely unaware that they should have, at the very least, their own Public Liability Insurance and yet seem to remain in regular work despite this.

In a nutshell: if (when) this industry winds up operating completely under PAYE, the cost of engaging the services of freelancers will rise by around 25%. The employers (as they will legally then become) will be lumbered with employer's NI at 12%, holiday pay at 8.3% and even statutory sick pay, along with the costs of providing insurance, tools, PPE, etc. There will also be several back tax bills flying around, most of which would be capable of sinking many of the small companies which make up the majority of our industry.

Also, if they become employees, most freelancers are almost certain to start asking questions about hourly pay, or just how long 'a day' actually is and what the overtime deal is after that. This will make it impossible for hire companies to give a fixed price for a job in advance. As more companies switched to PAYE there would be a diminishing financial incentive for freelancers to maintain their own insurance, etc. and we might see the final push into PAYE coming from the freelancers themselves. Television and Theatre style unionisation might then be just a short step away (heaven forbid!).

How might those who use freelancers pay for this 25% increase? There are three possible options as we see it:

1. They swallow the cost themselves somehow.
2. They pass it on to their clients.
3. They get the freelancers pay for it in some way.

Draft Freelancer Contract

The draft freelancer contract in this document (see page 97) offers some guidance as to the terms and conditions under which freelancer's services should be engaged in order to allow them to be classed as self-employed. It also negates the need for a purchase order (unless the client specifically wishes to issue one). It is not just a list of rules, but a flexible document with plenty of empty spaces to fill with numbers, so that there is room for financial negotiation and the traditional haggling.

But it is still not the end of the story. If a production or the contract schedule lists precise times when the freelancer will perform their duties, or if a long list of terms is laid down by the client, then the freelancer can still be classed as an employee. Not only that, but the quote supplied by the freelancer should, strictly speaking, include PDs, travel, accommodation and subsistence. There are further bitter pills in the contract to be swallowed by both sides. Clients (companies) must accept a freelancer's right to assign the actual labour to a third party, as this is another HMCR 'test' of true self-employment.

Freelancers must also have the right to cancellation fees. Freelancers themselves meanwhile must take fuller (in fact complete) responsibility for the way of life they have chosen and start to run it on a more businesslike basis. People who decide to use this document should keep themselves up to date with the tax regulations regarding self-employment, which are frequently 'amended'. One up to date source of information on the general subject of direct tax is *The Tax Investigations Reporter* published by CCH Publications.

At a yearly subscription of around £550 + VAT & p+p it is beyond the reach of many, although the publishers claim it will put your knowledge on a par with that of a Tax Inspector and some larger companies may find it a worthwhile investment.

Another thing to consider is that HMCR in general often operates on a 'local' basis, with each tax office interpreting the rules in its own slightly different way. What may be acceptable to one tax office may be completely out of the question to the next. The HMCR have also said that they intend to "look behind" contracts, probably by mounting aspect inquiries into individuals.

In other words it will not matter what is in the contract because the Revenue will be looking at what you actually do, rather than what the contract says you do. Whether you actually want to raise this issue with your own tax office is a matter for you, but it's probably best to speak to your accountants instead. Don't forget: it was a request for formal guidance from the Revenue which eventually brought PAYE to TV and Film.

We must accept as an industry that these are rules we cannot change.

They apply to all industries, everywhere in the UK and our industry is no exception.

They affect every freelancer and everybody who uses freelancers, not just hire companies, but production companies, managers, promoters, producers, agents – just about anyone you can think of really. It is the users of freelancers who have the most to lose, as they not only have to use investigative means to ensure the self-employed person is up to date with their Tax and NI payments, but will pick up the financial penalties if this is not done and they are caught. Yet it is basically the freelancer's duty to ensure that they operate and are engaged under conditions which allow them to be classed as truly self-employed and to state what those conditions are. However, most freelancers don't do this for fear that their services will not be engaged so often, if indeed ever again. All you hire companies, management companies and promoters, be honest: whose services do you engage most readily: the freelancer who says "Yes!", or the freelancer who says…

"Give me as full a description of the gig as possible and I will send you a quote, along with two copies of my contract stating my terms and conditions, signed by me, which should hopefully allow me to be classed as a self-employed person. If you accept my quote for the job, then sign both contracts and return one copy to me, along with a purchase order if you wish."

Well?

Out of touch with reality? That's the way we have to start operating, not some time in the future, but right now, if we want to avoid the nightmares described above and keep the financial benefits of Self Employment for us all. Don't forget, financial records must be kept for the last six years and are open to inspection by HMCR at any time.

If the industry does wind up on PAYE, it might be the freelancers who 'win' in the long term. Even though they will lose over a third of their money (including National Insurance) at source and most (but possibly not all) of their tax deductible benefits, they will gain a whole new load of rights and protection at their employer's expense and be able to unload many costly responsibilities onto them as well.

They may even get odd tax rebates rather than regular tax bills and let's face it: with the way state pensions are going it probably wouldn't hurt any freelancer to start paying some 'proper' National Insurance right now. It's true that the employers will pay for it dearly, but PAYE could give them the kind of control over their workforce that they really want and maybe actually need if they are to comply with the Health & Safety regulations. PAYE might even serve to level the playing field a little in some ways and lead to some general improvements in industry standards. Maybe we should not be so quick to rubbish PAYE after all.

The industry stands at a crossroads on the subject of PAYE and it is the Industry that will ultimately choose which path it takes, either through action or complacency. Can we maintain the self-employed status within our industry? Do we want to? Or do we just accept that the party is over and it's time to change?

The bottom line is that if you engage freelancers on a daily or hourly rate then you are probably their employer and you bear all the responsibilities of an employer. If you're a freelancer and you work for daily or hourly rates then you are almost certainly an employee and not self-employed. In both cases there is "no business risk" to the freelancer, and the HMCR do not consider a show or tour being cancelled as being a "business risk". The advice is to get professional advice now before it's too late!

The Limited Company Option

With the introduction of IR35 by HMCR, becoming a partnership or limited company no longer provides an automatic defence against taxation at source for freelancers nowadays. For example: imagine that Finbarr Fader sets up a company called "Finbarr Fader Ltd". Finbarr Fader Esq becomes an employee of that company. If Finbarr Fader Ltd gets a contract and sends Finbarr Fader Esq (the only employee of the company) out to do the job, say for a production company, HMCR may (under HMCR35) look at that transaction and ask: "If Finbarr Fader Ltd did not exist would Finbarr Fader Esq be classed as an employee of the production company?" If the answer is YES then the Revenue will probably consider that any fee paid to Finbarr Fader Ltd should be subject to Tax and NIC. HMCR will claim this back from Finbarr Fader Ltd, together with any interest and penalties due! Finbarr Fader Ltd will be charged for the extra tax and NIC's. The Revenue will not claim against Finbarr Fader Esq himself unless his company defaults on the payment of Tax and NIC's due.

The company (Finbarr Fader Ltd.) is allowed to deduct 5% from the total fees charged for the work carried out and the reminder will be a deemed salary in the hands of Finbarr Fader Esq. The company must calculate the relevant employer's NI which is deducted from the total (i.e. the 95%) to arrive at the gross salary in Finbarr Fader Esq.'s hands. This will then be subject to deduction of employee's NI and PAYE whether or not the monies have been paid to F. F. If the partnership or company has ignored IR 35, then corporation tax will have been paid on the profits of the company, and if the Revenue subsequently investigate and apply IR 35 the partnership or company will be required to pay the additional PAYE and NI on the deemed salary plus interest and penalties. This could be some years along the line and amount to a very considerable sum.

It is worth noting that some of the work carried out by F F Ltd could fall under IR 35 and some not. There are also considerations regarding year-ends and timing that must be taken into consideration. Professional advice should be sought at an early date, rather than at some time in the future when the proverbial has already hit the fan!

In these self-employment 'situations', the responsibility is for Finbarr Fader to prove he is genuinely self-employed and one of the 'acid tests' is: "is it possible for Finbarr Fader to make a loss as well as a profit? Does Finbarr Fader take any "business risk?" In this situation Finbarr Fader Ltd is known as an "Intermediary Company" and it is these Intermediaries that the HMCR want to stomp all over with IR 35.

A Simple Guide to Self Employment

Interpretation

In this document the following words are used:

Self-employed contractor – a person supplying goods or services, a small organisation with a single person acting as a sole trader. A self-employed contractor is often referred to as a "freelancer" but this is not the correct term as a freelancer can also be paid under PAYE for all or some of the work he or she carries out for his or her clients.

Client – customer or the person or organisation contracting the goods or services, usually the organisation paying the invoice.

Introduction

A self-employed contractor is contracted by a client to provide goods and or services and is therefore a trade supplier. As a trade supplier there is no entitlement to any benefits such as sick pay, holiday pay, pensions, Per Diems (PDs) and benefits provided by the client to their employees.

A self-employed contractor should have made adequate provision for insurance covering the scope of work they have been contracted to provide, typically this should include Public and Employees Liability, Contractors All Risks covering plant and equipment, and Travel and Medical insurance. The client may stipulate the amount of cover required as in some contractual situations the amounts of cover must be the same amongst all contractors – this is especially so in the case of Public Liability Insurance.

Self-employed contractors also have their own responsibilities under the Health and Safety at Work Act 1974 (HASAWA), and will be required to make adequate provision for personal protective equipment (PPE), risk assessments, method statements, safe systems of work, first aid, accident reporting, etc but this is where it gets confusing because the HSE consider it "good practice" for an employer to provide PPE and training for the self-employed contractors they use and HMCR have agreed that in doing so the self-employed status will not be affected.

Self-employed contractors are advised to have a contract between themselves and any clients with whom they are engaged to provide services for.

A contract between a self-employed contractor and a client is a contract to supply services, it is not a contract of employment or contract of service. It will assist in establishing a self-employed contractors status and will go some way in protecting both the parties in the event of a dispute.

Any contract should be issued by the self-employed contractor to a client stating the self-employed contractor's terms and conditions of business, a contract issued by a client – e.g. a service company or an artist/artist management company, to a self-employed contractor may be construed as a contract of employment.

A sample contract is attached at the end of these guidance notes for use by the self-employed contractor.

Areas marked < ...... > indicate any details that need entering – this may be a name, date, monetary sum or figure.

These should be completed at the time of negotiation with the client.

The list of clauses contained within the sample contract are by no means an exhaustive list; the self-employed contractor may wish to add additional clauses to suit their own particular needs. Additionally they may find that the client wishes additional clauses to be added or for changes made to existing clauses.

This is only to be expected but it is advised that legal advice be sought if the self-employed contractor is not 100% certain of the meaning or validity of a particular clause.

It is also suggested that any paragraphs, lines or words that are struck out or altered should be initialled by both parties and dated.

The notes that follow give guidance as to what HMCR and the Health and Safety Executive (HSE) consider to be a self-employed contractor but each and every case is different. For further advice contact your local area tax office.

It cannot be stressed to often that a self-employed contractor is not an employee and holds all the responsibilities of a person running their own business. A self-employed contractor is in fact considered to be an employer by the HSE and HMCR as he employs himself; he has all the responsibilities of both an employer and employee!

What Is Self-Employment?

The HSE consider that self-employment is someone who employs themselves. They may also be an employer.

This same view is adopted by HM tax inspector as a definition of who is "self-employed" as opposed to an employee but with many additional indicators.

HM tax inspectors are also asking self-employed persons if they are allowed to put someone in to do the job on their behalf, they consider that self-employed contractors must be allowed to assign a job. Obviously, this kind of substitution does not hold with employment, similarly, a self-employed contractor does not work under supervision.

If you work for an employer who covers you under their Employers Liability Insurance then the chances are you are an employee even if you pay your own tax and National Insurance contribution. This is even more the case if you work under supervision such as a "stage hand/local crew" person may do.

Employers need to take care as well. You may end up with a large bill for National Insurance Contributions for your self-employed contractors who you thought were paying their own N.I. contributions. This has already happened to at least one company in our industry and it cost them a fortune!

Clients undertaking the services of self-employed contractors are advised to keep evidence of the defining criteria used to determine "self-employed" status. It is no longer acceptable for a self-employed contractor just to state that they are a "self-employed" and provide a self-employment reference number.

Typical defining criteria will consist of a questionnaire about the self-employed contractor, the services provided, qualifications and training information, bank details, tax and national insurance details, written evidence of your trading status e.g. accountants letter or letter from HMCR and Insurance details. Once the client has satisfied themselves of your "self-employed" status they will treat your invoice for payment as trade invoices. Otherwise they have to treat you as an employee and deduct tax and NI at source.

It is very important to ascertain a self-employed contractors status as to whether they are in fact employed or self-employed. No client in their right mind should use self-employed contractors unless they carry insurance suitable for the scope of work they have been contracted to carry out.

If the client (as an employer) intends to cover individuals under their own employers/public liability insurance they may then become an employee of the client who then has to take all the responsibilities of an employer.

Clients, production managers, crew chief/bosses take note. You may have employees you did not think you had together with all the responsibilities for health and safety, tax, national insurance, sick pay, holiday pay and working time regulations.

The more you provide for self-employed contractors, the more likely that they may be classed as your employees.

Full details of assessing employee or self-employed status can be found in the section entitled **"IR 56 – Guidance on Employment Status"**.

One of the checks that employers can make to ascertain that the "labour only contractors" they intend to appoint are genuine self-employed persons is by getting them to quote for the jobs available and not offering a weekly, daily or hourly rate of pay.

Strictly speaking the quote from a self-employed person should include things like transport, accommodation, *per diems* and subsistence.

Quoting for a job uses "entrepreneurial skills" and is an 'acid test' for true self-employment but even then it may be possible to do the occasional job for a daily or hourly rate, for instance, if it proves to be extremely difficult to quote a price to do the whole job because until you start you don't know how long it's going to take or what is involved. This seems to be acceptable as long as it's only occasional and does not represent the majority of your work. Purchase orders, invoices and contract schedules should never include daily, weekly or hourly rates of pay, the hours to be worked or start and finish times. The fact a tour, a show or an event may be cancelled is not considered a "entrepreneurial risk" or to be using "entrepreneurial skills".

Invoices raised by self-employed contractors should be all encompassing and typically use phrases like "For goods and services provided on ABC event as per our (verbal) quotation". It is suggested invoices are not split into days, hours, weeks etc. unless used to indicate additional services outside of the original quote, or as suggested in the paragraph above, if it is difficult to quote due the nature of the contracted work.

A number of companies in our industry who use the services of self-employed contracts are now insisting these self-employed persons become "limited companies" before they will use their services. These companies often claim that there are advantages to the self-employed to trader as a limited company. The advice of various accountants was that it was a disadvantage to becoming a limited company unless your business has a turn over of a least £100,000 per year and the responsibility under the HMCR 35 regulations all rest with the self-employed contractor.

The only people who can really decide if you are genuinely self-employed or not are HMCR and even then it's quite possible for each local area office to give a different definition and ruling on each case.

All the information I have given here acts only as indicators but it's a fair bet that the more indicators you have pointing towards self-employment, the more likely you are to be "self-employed".

Employers must remember that self-employed persons are not "short term employees" and must not be treated as such.

Employment status is not a matter of choice. People are self-employed if they are in business on their own account and bear the responsibility for its success or failure.

HMCR quote that "The tax rules for self-employed people are designed to reflect the day-to-day transactions of the true risk-taking entrepreneur. Genuine self-employment is about being in business on one's own account and not simply applying a label of self-employment".

The self-employed are advised to use the services of a charted accountant to assist and advise them on their financial affairs and to keep business and personal bank accounts separate. You are required to register as self-employed with HM Customs and Revenue within three months of starting work as a self-employed person. The simplest way of paying National Insurance by a self-employed person is by direct debit.

Bear in mind that because you are self-employed in one job doesn't necessarily mean you will be in your next job.

TEMPLATE CONTRACT TO PROVIDE GOODS AND SERVICES

THIS AGREEMENT is made the < .... > day of < .... >
BETWEEN   < ....
>of : <...>(The Supplier)
and<... >of:
<..
....>(The Client)

CONTRACT DETAILS : CONTRACT NO: < ....>

EVENT, PRODUCTION OR TOUR:
<.. >

DURATION OF THE AGREEMENT: < ....>
to <........................>

1. The Supplier agrees to supply goods/services in accordance with the Schedule attached hereto or as subsequently agreed in writing by the parties hereto.

2. It is hereby agreed that prior to the signing hereof The Client has had ample opportunity to examine The Supplier's Terms of Business attached hereto and shall be deemed to have unequivocally accepted them.

3. The total contract price shall be <£................ > plus VAT (if applicable)

4. The terms of payment are:

5. In the event of cancellation of this Agreement by The Client and without prejudice to any rights hereunder or under the Terms of Business attached hereto, The Client will indemnify The Supplier as

a result of such cancellation for < .... >% of the contract price. Interest at a rate of < ..... >% per month is liable to be charged on any outstanding balances.

6. It is a fundamental terms of this agreement that the stipulations as to payment contained be fully adhered to by The Client (including an absolute requirement of payment to be made within the times stipulated but subject to the proviso contained in Condition 4) and if for any reason The Client shall be in breach of such stipulations The Supplier shall have the right at its absolute and sole discretion and without prejudice to its other rights hereunder forthwith and without notice to dismantle remove or otherwise bring to an end any works service goods or other things supplied by the supplier hereunder and to terminate forthwith this agreement and be under no further liability hereunder to provide any of the services or goods herein agreed.

Signed for and on behalf of)

The Supplier)

Signed for and on behalf of)

The Client)

IN ADDITION TO SIGNING THE AGREEMENT, THE CLIENT IS REQUESTED TO INITIAL ALL PAGES OF THIS AGREEMENT, THE TERMS OF BUSINESS AND SCHEDULES, IN THE TOP RIGHT HAND CORNER

TERMS OF BUSINESS

1. All services and goods supplied by The Supplier are subject to the terms set out herein and in the Agreement attached unless varied in writing by the parties. The signing of the Agreement shall be deemed to be acceptance of these Terms of Business.

2. All works, goods and services shall be supplied by The Supplier to a good and workman like standard in accordance with the Schedule which is annexed hereto so far as the circumstances shall reasonably allow. The Client shall ensure that the Schedule complies in all respects with their requirements, or any authority or any other person or entity involved. The Supplier reserves the right to alter or amend the Schedule at any time if in the absolute discretion of The Supplier the needs of safety so require.

3. The Client must ensure that all necessary licences, consents and authorities to stage the event/s have been obtained and shall indemnify The Supplier in respect of any liability costs or claims arising there from.

4. The contract price shall be paid strictly in accordance with the terms of payment contained in the Agreement.

5. The Client shall for the duration of the agreement place in force public liability insurance to a minimum indemnity of <£ ....> and shall produce evidence of such insurance at the request of The Supplier.

6. The Supplier shall for the duration of the agreement place in force public liability insurance to a minimum indemnity of <£ ....> and shall produce evidence of such insurance at the request of The Client.

7. Unless listed in The Suppliers Terms and Conditions, The Client

shall be responsible for supplying the items or services listed is the schedules attached hereto at no cost The Supplier.

The Client shall ensure that all equipment provided by The Supplier is fully protected from and insured against all risks (including but not limited to, theft and malicious acts in respect to equipment) and shall produce evidence of such insurance with The Supplier's interest noted thereon at the request of The Supplier.

9. The Supplier shall not be liable in respect of any damage caused to the site(s) or venue(s) either during the event/s or as a result of the erection and/or dismantling of equipment and services unless such damage results from the negligent act or admission of The Supplier, the servants, agents or sub-contractors, or persons for whom they are responsible.

10. The Supplier shall so far as is reasonably practicable follow the Health and Safety rules and arrangements as set out in The Clients Health and Safety Policy.

11. Unless otherwise agreed in writing by both parties to this Agreement, The Supplier acknowledges and accepts that:
The Client will not be providing First-Aid cover for The Supplier or for The Suppliers employees for the duration of this agreement. The Supplier will be responsible for making First-Aid arrangements according to the standards set by the Health and Safety (First-Aid) Regulations 1981 for The Supplier and for The Suppliers employees.

12. The Supplier shall retain the right to assign this contract.

13. The Supplier shall keep secret and shall not use or disclose and shall use his/her best endeavours to prevent the use or disclosure by or to any person any of The Client's or The Client's clients confidential information which came to his/her knowledge during the engagement. The restriction shall apply during and after The Suppliers engagement without any time limit but shall cease to apply to information or knowledge which the Supplier establishes

has in it's entirety become public knowledge otherwise than through the unauthorised disclosure or other breach of the Suppliers part of that restriction. Confidential information means all confidential information relating to the organisation, finances, business activities and private activities of the Client, The Client's client and either of their employees and agents, suppliers or advisors.
The Supplier further agrees not to use any information gleaned during the term of this Agreement to directly or indirectly solicit business from any of The Client's clients.

14. The Supplier shall not be liable for any breach of the Agreement or terms hereof where such a breach was caused by or substantially contributed to by any cause beyond the control of the Supplier including (without limitation) Act of God insurrections riot civil commotion's Government or other enforceable regulations embargoes explosions strikes labour disputes fire and exceptionally adverse weather. The Supplier's sub-contractors shall be deemed to be parties to the Agreement for the purpose of obtaining the protection of this clause and The Client shall indemnify The Supplier in respect of any claim by a third party in respect of which liability is excluded by this clause provided always that The Supplier shall use its best endeavours to prevent such a breach or mitigate the effects thereof.

15. If The Client shall make any assignment for the benefit of its creditors, commit and/or fail to inform The Supplier of any act of bankruptcy or if, being a limited company, shall suffer any receiver of its assets to be appointed or upon commencement of any winding up or upon failure to pay any sum due to The Supplier whether due under this contract or otherwise upon other breach of contract by The Client, The Supplier shall be entitled to cease work immediately and to dismantle remove or otherwise bring to an end any works service goods or other things supplied by The Supplier hereunder. Upon ceasing work dismantling removing or otherwise bringing to an end any works service goods or other things supplied by The Supplier hereunder, this contract shall be deemed to have been terminated but without affecting any pre-existing rights of the parties

including The Supplier's right to receive payment of the full price of the contract without deduction.

16. Any contract to which these terms apply shall be construed in accordance with the laws of England and the parties agree to accept the jurisdiction of the courts of England.

SCHEDULES

The Supplier will provide for the duration of The Agreement:

The Client will provide for the duration of The Agreement:

IF IT IS PROPOSED TO USE SUBSTITUTE CONTRACTORS THIS ADDITIONAL CLAUSE MAY BY USED IN THE CONTRACT

1.   ..... *(insert name of contractor)* may offer a substitute contractor in his place, providing that all the following conditions are met:

- the services provided by the proposed substitute remain as detailed in the schedule
- the Client is satisfied that any substitute is suitable. In practice, this will mean that he possesses the necessary qualifications, experience and indemnity insurance to fulfill the terms of the contract
- the Client is satisfied that the proposed substitute has sufficient resources to perform the contract to a sufficiently high standard
- the Client is satisfied that the intended substitute will comply with its rules on confidentiality, health, safety and security
- the costs associated with any training of the substitute and handover period will be met by ..... *(insert name of contractor)*.

Consent to the proposed substitution is given to .... *(insert name of contractor)* in writing first.

The Client reserves the right to refuse a proposed substitute only if the substitute does not have the necessary skills and cannot fulfill the contractual requirements.

CONTRACTS
The Department for Business, Enterprise & Regulatory Reform
The contract of employment

A contract of employment is an agreement entered into by an employer and an employee under which they have certain mutual obligations.

If no contract of employment exists beforehand, one will come into existence as soon as an employee starts work and, by doing so, demonstrates that he or she accepts the job on the terms offered by the employer. The contract need not be in writing, unless it is a contract of apprenticeship (employers should note however that a contract of apprenticeship may be found by the courts to be implied even if it is not in writing). Its terms can be written, oral, implied or a mixture of all three. Implied terms might include those that are too obvious to be expressly agreed – for example, a term that the employee must accept reasonable instructions from the employer – those that are necessary to make the contract workable and those that are established by custom and practice in the particular organisation or industry concerned.

Employed or self-employed?

As already discussed, whether someone is an employee working under a contract of employment or a self-employed person working under a contract to provide services depends upon the true nature of the agreement entered into by the parties. If the employer has a duty to provide work, controls when and how it is done, supplies the tools or other equipment needed to do it and pays tax and national insurance contributions on the worker's behalf, then it is likely that the worker is an employee. If, on the other hand, the worker can decide whether or not to accept work and how to carry it out, makes his or her own arrangements for holidays or sickness absences, pays his or her own tax and national insurance contributions and is free to do the same type of work for more than one employer at the same time, this points towards the person being self-employed. The fact that a worker is described (either by himself or herself or by the employer) as being self-employed does not necessarily mean that this is actually so. Neither does the fact that the worker does the job on the employer's premises or from his or her own home determine the issue. The important question is whether or not the worker is genuinely in business on his or her own account. If a dispute arises in which employment status is in doubt, this can be considered as a preliminary issue by the Employment Tribunal or the court concerned, taking into account all factors relevant to the case.

Written statement of employment particulars

All employees taken on for one month or more are entitled by law to be given, within two months of the date the employment starts, a written statement setting out the main particulars. This statement will not necessarily cover every aspect of the contract, but will constitute important evidence of the principal terms and conditions. Further information about the right to a written statement can be found in *Written Statement of Employment Particulars*.

Variation of contract

The contract of employment is binding on both parties. This means that it is unlawful for one party to vary the terms and conditions in the contract without the agreement of the other. The contract itself may, however, include provisions allowing the employer to make important changes – for example, requiring the employee to move to a different place of work or to undertake a different type of work. In the case of a change covered by a provision of this kind, there is no variation of the terms and conditions in the contract and the change will be lawful.

It is always open to either party to seek to renegotiate the terms and conditions with the other. A variation may be made by agreement between the employer and the employee. It may alternatively result from a variation by collective agreement, where the contract itself (either expressly or by implication, such as through long standing custom and practice) provides for this.

A collective agreement is one made between, on the one hand, an employer or an association representing employers and, on the other, a trade union representing employees. The contract may provide for its terms to be varied by a particular collective agreement even if the employee is not a member of a trade union (so that, for example, collectively negotiated pay agreements can be incorporated into all employees' contracts).

An employee's written statement of employment particulars must specify any collective agreements that directly affect his or her terms and conditions (including, where the employer is not a party, the identities of the parties). If a variation of contract affects one or more of the terms and conditions required by law to be covered in the employee's written statement of employment particulars, then the employee must be given written notification of this. The notification must be given as soon as possible, and at any rate no later than one month after the variation is made.

It should be noted that if an employee finds a variation of contract unsatisfactory but nevertheless continues to work under the new terms and conditions without making his or her objections known to the employer, he or she could after a time be deemed to have implicitly accepted it and it would then become incorporated into the contract.

Refusal by employee to authorise variation

If the employer wishes to vary the terms and conditions of employment and the employee, having been consulted, objects to the variation, then the employer may decide to terminate the contract by dismissing the employee. As usual in the event of dismissal, the appropriate statutory or contractual notice (or pay in lieu of notice) would have to be given and any other contractual obligations relating to the termination of employment would have to be fulfilled The employer would then be free to offer the job on different terms and conditions either to the dismissed employee or to another applicant. If the dismissed employee considered the employer's actions to have been unfair, he or she would be entitled to make a complaint of unfair dismissal to an employment tribunal – provided that he or she had completed a qualifying period of at least one year's continuous service.

This applies to dismissals taking place on or after 1 June 1999: previously two years' continuous service was necessary. Such complaints must normally be made within three months of the date the employment ended. The tribunal would consider all the circumstances of the case in deciding whether or not the dismissal was in fact unfair. These would include the employer's reasons for wishing to vary the terms and conditions – overriding business considerations, for example, might make the dismissal fair – and the employee's reasons for opposing the variation.

If an employer attempts simply to impose a variation of contract on an employee without the employee's agreement, this will be a breach of contract. The employee may have various means of redress available in law. These are described in the following sections of this document.

Breach of contract claims by employees

There are a number of factors that a dismissed employee making a claim for breach of employment contract may wish to bear in mind in deciding which of the two alternatives – employment tribunal or civil court – to use. For example, the employment tribunals provide a generally speedier and more informal means of redress than the civil courts for the resolution of employment disputes, and their procedures have been designed to make it unnecessary for the parties to incur the cost of legal representation.

On the other hand, employment tribunal claims must be made within three months of the date on which the employment ended (or, if that is not reasonably practicable, within such further period as the tribunal considers reasonably practicable), whereas civil court claims may be made up to a much longer time limit of six years from the date on which the breach of contract occurred. Another consideration might be that employment tribunal awards for an employer's breach of contract are subject to an upper limit, currently £25,000, whereas civil court awards may reflect the full amount of the damages suffered by the dismissed employee.

Breach of contract claims by employers

If an employer suffers a measurable financial loss because one of his or her employees breaches the contract of employment, or any other contract connected with employment, then the employer is entitled to seek damages by making a breach of contract claim. The normal forum for pursuing such a claim is a county court or other civil court. A claim may be made in an employment tribunal instead, but only if it is in response to a breach of contract claim that an employee has already made to an employment tribunal and that has not since been settled or with-drawn. In addition, the claim:

- must arise or be outstanding on the termination of employment of the employee against whom it is made;

- and to relationships of the special categories listed above in respect to employees' claims.

If the dismissed employee withdraws his or her breach of contract claim after the employer has made a claim, the employer's claim can still be considered by the employment tribunal. Employment tribunal claims by employers must normally be made within six weeks of the date on which the employer (or other respondent) receives from the tribunal a copy of the dismissed employee's originating application (or, if that is not reasonably practicable, within such further period as the tribunal considers reasonably practicable). Civil court claims may be made up to a much longer time limit of six years from the date on which the breach of contract occurred. Employment tribunal awards for a breach of contract by an employee are subject to an upper limit, currently £25,000, whereas civil court awards may reflect the full amount of the damages suffered by the employer.

Constructive unfair dismissal

If an employer breaches an employee's contract of employment in a fundamental way, which effectively indicates that he or she no longer intends to be bound by its terms, the employee may be entitled to resign and to regard himself or herself as having been forced to take that step in response to the employer's behaviour. This is known as constructive dismissal. If the constructively dismissed employee considers the dismissal to have been unfair, he or she will be entitled to make an unfair dismissal complaint to an employment tribunal in the same way as if the employer had expressly dismissed him or her for objecting to a variation of the agreed terms and conditions of employment. Again, the right to make an employment tribunal complaint on these grounds is subject to a one year qualifying period of continuous service. The tribunal would first consider whether or not there was a constructive dismissal and then, if there was, decide whether or not the dismissal was in fact unfair in all the circumstances.

IR 35 – IGNORANCE IS NO DEFENCE

When, in the 1999 budget, the Chancellor announced he was introducing measures which would stop companies laying off workers on a Friday and taking them back on the Monday on a contract basis, so depriving the workers of their statutory rights, sick pay, maternity pay etc. there could have been few who would have disagreed with the sentiment.

Some months later this altruistic statement proved to be somewhat less than transparent – it was in fact a new stealth tax aimed at increasing revenue in the Treasury coffers. The measure has become known as IR 35, and, according to the Paymaster General of the time, Dawn Primarolo, could affect as many as 90,000 small businesses in the UK, and other estimates are higher.

Will it affect your business? Do you know what IR 35 is? Do you think it will only apply to IT and engineering? You could be in for a nasty shock.

IR 35, in a nutshell, could apply to anyone who has at least a 5% share in their limited company or partnership and physically carries out the company contracts themselves personally, to their clients.

This could be in IT, it could be engineering but it could also include lighting designers, sound engineers, back-line technicians, riggers, catering and wardrobe crew, dental hygienists, milkmen, drivers, builders, lecturers, training personnel, welders, electricians, maintenance fitters, in fact anyone who provides personal services to the client through their own company.

You may contract direct with your customer or you may contract through an agency, it will not matter. If HMCR decide to investigate your status they will apply HMCR standard employment tests to each and every one of your contracts to establish if you are really what they call 'self-employed' or whether you are in fact a 'disguised employee' of your client company.

And if they decide you are in fact a disguised employee, they will demand that you pay Tax and NI on 95 % of your total company income from the contract, after allowing you to deduct only Professional Indemnity Insurance costs and those limited expenses you could have claimed under self-employment had you really been an employee. The remaining 5% will be allowed to cover all your business expenses including insurances, accountancy fees, etc. You will no longer be able to make capital investments in the way normal companies do.

Any money you choose to leave in your company will be money on which you will have paid Income Tax and National Insurance which cannot be reclaimed against capital investments as you would Corporation Tax.

You will not even be able to make tax deductible company donations to charity. You will no longer be able to retain profits for lean times as under IR 35 there can be no profits, 95% of income is paid out as 'deemed salary'.

If HMCR decide you are a disguised employee you will not of course still not be able to claim sickness benefit, etc from your disguised employer as HMCR specifically states it does not alter your company status and is a personal tax on the individual. You will still be employed by your own company.

The only difference is you will not be paying the same tax and NI as an employee of your disguised employer. What employee also pays employers NI on their earnings?

Dawn Primarolo has stated it will be relatively easy for an individual to assess their status and if in doubt there are facilities to submit your contract to IR 35 status inspectors. Anyone who has looked at the HMCR employment status manuals will know they are far from simple and any decision by a status inspector will be far from objective. Indeed there is a specific instance of one contract receiving two assessments from the HM, one passed and one failed. This evidence was presented and accepted by the HMCR in court at the Judicial Review.

To make matters worse no business has received any communication from the HMCR to explain the new legislation. It has been almost exclusively publicised on the HMCR website. The result is the IT contract companies who use the web all the time, quickly became aware of the new laws and mounted a very vocal opposition to it. The British press perpetuated the myth that only IT were affected, as, in the main, did MP's, but every day more people who work through personal services companies find out they too could be caught.

If you supply your expertise to your clients are you sure IR 35 will not affect you? If you suspect it might or decide it does not and HMCR decide otherwise you could be in for a hefty tax bill and penalties some years down the line when HMCR decides to call.

Detailed official information on IR 35 can be found on HMCR website.

IR 56 – Guidance on Employment Status

This guidance is the same criteria (IR 56) used by HMCR to establish employment/self-employment status, the same criteria are also used to establish a person's status under the IR 35 Tax Regulations.

This information must be used for guidance only, the final decision on a person's employment status can only be decided by HMCR office, even then it is not clear cut and one office can give a different ruling to another on the same case.

A company can provide a self-employed person with Training and PPE with-out affecting that persons self-employed status. It is in fact considered good practice to treat self-employed contractors as employees for health and safety purposes but it must be remembered this is not a legal requirement and is not enforceable

	Detail as appropriate	Tick as appropriate	
		E	SE
Are there people doing similar duties? If "YES" are they employed or self-employed? Has a formal Tax Office ruling been given and if so by who? If "employed", what are the differences in the terms of engagement?	YES/NO	E	SE
Was the individual previously employed by you? If so, when was the change? What are the differences in the terms of engagement?		YES	NO
Did the individuals claim to be self-employed at the start of the present engagement?		NO	YES
Does he have a Self Employed reference number? If so, what is it?		NO	YES
Does he have an accountant? If so, what is the name and address?		NO	YES
How was the work obtained? If it was advertised, can I have a copy? If unavailable, what was said in the advertisement? Was the individual interviewed? What information was given?	YES/NO		

	Detail as appropriate	Tick as appropriate	
		E	SE
Is there a written contract, letter of agreement or other correspondence setting out terms and conditions? If so, can I have copies?	YES/NO		
If there is no written contracts or other correspondence covering the engagement what oral agreements were made between the parties?			
If work is sub-standard, can the individual be told to do it again at his own expense?		NO	YES
Can the individual be moved from job to job if priorities change?		YES	NO
Who decides where the work is done?		Co	I
Who decides what is to be done?		Co	I
Who decides how the work is done? What written instructions or other guidance has been given to the individual? Has the worker a particular skill or experience which means no-one needs to tell him how to do his work?		Co NO	YES
Who decides when the work is to be done? Are there set hours? Are there arrangements for meal breaks?		Co YES YES	I No NO
What are the arrangements regarding holiday pay? Do you pay the individual holiday pay?		YES	YES
Do you pay the individual sick pay?		YES	NO

	Detail as appropriate	Tick as appropriate	
		E	**SE**
Must the individual do the work himself or can he use a stand-in? If stand-ins can be used, was there a specific provision to this effect when the individual commenced? In what circumstances can stand-ins be provided? Who make the decision to engage them? Who recruits them? Who pays them? Have any actually been provided? Is so, under what circumstances?		SELF NO Co Co Co NO	S/IN YES I I I YES
What equipment is necessary to do the job? Who provides it? Who is responsible for the equipments upkeep?		Co Co	I I
Has the individual invested any capital in the business?		NO	YES
Is there any chance that the individual may make a loss on the engagement?		NO	YES
Does the individual have to meet the cost of expenses, for example telephone, office stationary etc?		NO	YES
Does the individual pay for special insurance cover such as public liability?		NO	YES
On what basis is payment calculated, e.g. hourly, weekly, daily, by the piece etc? How is it paid? e.g. cash, cheque, etc. Is overtime paid? What is the frequency of payment? Does the individual provide receipts? Is the individual registered for VAT?		YES NO NO	NO YES YES

	Detail as appropriate	Tick as appropriate	
		E	**SE**
Is payment made for expenses?		YES	NO
Is a company car provided?		YES	NO
Is the individual eligible to join the company's pension scheme?		YES	NO
Is the company under any obligation to provide or offer further work?		YES	NO
Is the individual under a similar obligation to offer or provide further services? If so, how is the work/services offered or accepted?		YES	NO
Has work ever been refused by the individual?		NO	YES
Is there any exclusivity, i.e. can the individual only work for you for the duration of this engagement?		YES	NO
If there are no restrictions, is there any scope for the individual to provide services to others?		NO	YES
Does the individual provide similar services to other concerns?		NO	YES
Is it clear that work has been provided on a continues basis?		YES	NO
How does the individual fit in with your company? Who is he answerable to? Is he responsible for the work of others and if so, are they employed or self-employed?			
Is the work self-contained, i.e. does the individual offer a specific service or produce a particular item?		NO	YES
Does the individual present himself to customers as a representative of your company? Does he have a business card and if so what is written on it?		YES	NO
Does the company have the right to dismissal? Is the individual entitled to a period of notice?	YES/NO	YES	NO

SELF-EMPLOYMENT in the Live Music and Events Industry

SIMPLIFIED CHECKLIST OF STATUS FACTORS

	EMPLOYMENT INDICATORS	SELF-EMPLOYMENT INDICATORS
Control	Control by another in the manner in which the work is performed.	No control by another over the manner in which the work is done.
Hours of Work	The person for whom the work is done lays down and defined hours of work.	The person performing the work is free to decide when he wishes to work.
Place of Work	The person performing the work works in premises owned by the person for whom he performs the work.	The person who performs the work decides where it will be performed.
Tools/Equipment	The person for whom the work is being done provides the tools and equipment.	The person performing the work provides his own tools and equipment.
Payment	The person for whom work is being done cannot generally withhold payment.	The person for whom the work is done is free to withhold payment until the work is performed as agreed.
Reward	The person performing the work does not bear the losses nor keep the profits.	The person performing the work bears the losses and keeps the profits.
Delegation of Duties	The person performing the work is restricted from delegating his work to another.	The person performing the work is free to delegate his duties to another.
Rectifying Work	The person performing the work does not correct unsatisfactory work in his own time and at his own expense.	The person performing the work corrects unsatisfactory work in his own time and at his own expense.
Risk	The person performing the work does not risk his own money in it.	The person performing the work risks his own money in the business.
Dismissal	The person for whom the work is done can dismiss.	The person for whom the work is done cannot dismiss the worker or cancel the work once the work is agreed, without compensation.

Some of the employment/self-employment indicators used above are stronger than others and therefore with this in mind, we have this simplified "Checklist of Status Factors", which splits the indicators into "strong" and "weak".

Strong indicators:

- Would you allow the worker to provide a substitute if necessary, payment of whom will be his responsibility?
- You are not obliged to provide the worker with work e.g. during slow periods?
- Can the worker turn down work?
- Does the worker also work for other contractors?
- Does the worker provide his own tools and equipment which are fundamental to the work being carried out? (Small hand tools would be a weaker indicator)?
- Does the worker have to put right any errors or supply replacement materials at his own expense?
- No company or employee benefits are provided to the worker including paid holidays, sick pay or redundancy entitlement?
- Does the worker provide his own indemnity cover?

Weak indicators:

- Does the contract specify that it is a contract for services?
- Is the basis of remuneration a fixed fee for work done rather than a rate per hour or day?
- Does the worker have headed notepaper and invoices and bill the company for work regularly done?
- Is the worker free to work his own hours?
- Does the worker have control over how and where the work is done?
- Is it clear to the other company workers that the individual concerned is a contract worker and self-employed?
- Can you only terminate the agreement for a serious breach of contract?

A "Yes" answer is indicative of self-employment while a "No" answer indicates employment.

TAX REGULATION – SECTION 660
What is Section 660 (s660a)?

Section 660 is also called the "married couples business tax". It mainly impacts on individuals operating their own service company (self-employed /freelancer). The term has caused a great deal of controversy and media attention as people have been caught with tax-bills dating back several years.

It has been suggested that half a million family businesses in the UK may face the tax. For decades businesses have reduced their tax bills by transferring profits, normally in the form of dividends, from earner to partner who is in the lower tax zone. Many people have received letters asking them to pay back money owed from years ago.

The Inland Revenue have hit many different companies, not only service companies. *The Times* has reported that TV stars and celebrities could be caught.

There are over 3.5 million 'small business' in the UK. It is suggested that around 70 per cent of UK businesses are run by people related either by blood or marriage.

It is a difficult issue for taxpayers as they have no way to calculate whether they are liable under 660, or how large that bill could be. As a rough estimation you could be at risk from Section 660 if:

- Your spouse owns ordinary shares in your company.
- Share profits with / pay dividends to any relatives, spouses or close partners who doesn't play an active role in the business.
- You pay dividends
- The amounts of money you and your spouse bring in to the company are not in proportion to the number of shares you own.

For many, the risk and uncertainty of Section 660 on top of IR 35 and other regulatory issues (not to mention the low rewards) is the final straw with some people choosing to close down businesses (particularly service company businesses) and look for a more secure trading vehicle.

Insurance

Insurance is not a "Get out of jail free" card – if you break the law your insurance will not cover you. Health and safety law is criminal law and it's impossible to insure against breaking criminal law! It is almost certain that your insurance will not be valid if you break any health and safety regulations.

Several trade associations and unions that have offered insurance packages as a member benefit have recently had the insurance withdrawn or rates increased by astronomic amounts. If a trade association or union offers such a package and the insurance was withdrawn then the trade association or union could be held responsible because a contract with members had been breached. This is a situation that is obviously unacceptable. Other organisations (and unions) offer very cheap insurance as a membership benefit but on further investigation it is often found that the insurance offered is only valid when working with members of the same organisation or union, when working only in the UK and when only doing work that is "recognised" by that organisation or union. These are unacceptable terms and restrictions that are almost impossible to comply with – don't be fooled by these cheap options and offers.

We must also remember that members of a trade association or union carry out a diverse range of jobs with various levels of risk and that no overall insurance package (of the type normally provided as a member benefit) will cover most of these situations.

Insurance companies now expect clients to meet minimum statutory health and safety requirements. A trade association or union is not be able to guarantee that members meet the minimum level of compliance to health and safety regulations that insurers will require for an adequate members package.

These days more people are aware of their legal responsibilities and do not want to take risks or be seen as 'cowboys'. They therefore insist the companies and contractors they use have all the necessary insurance cover. Don't be surprised if your turned down for work because you don't have the required insurance cover – "self-employed" crew should take note!

For the "self-employed" having the required insurance demonstrates a standard and a professional dedication to one's business. To not be insured indicates a "cowboy attitude" and a dangerous liability whose dubious services should not be considered.

Stagesafe urges clients to take out Public/Employers Liability insurance with insurers who are conversant with our industry and offer bespoke insurance packages.

The companies listed below offer bespoke insurance. Clients are advised to declare all types of work to be carried out to the insurers. Failure to declare may result in the invalidation of the insurance. For "self-employed" crew it is vital to ascertain if the insurance meets all your requirements. Ask simple questions like: Am I covered for loss or damage to my clients equipment? Am I covered for work at height? What countries does this insurance cover me in? Am I covered for electrical work? Am I covered for driving?

Self-employed (freelance) operators who either instruct or supervise other crew take on responsibility for the way their crew operates. If one of the crew you are supervising or instructing suffers an injury, it is then possible for them to sue you for damages even though you do not pay or employ them. Tour, stage, production managers and crew chiefs should make a special note of this advice. With the Employers Liability Cover, you will have legal representation for your defence and payment of damages, if they are awarded against you.

Those who use the services of contractors (including self-employed contractors often referred to as freelancers) should ensure that the contractors you use hold the same level of insurance as your company, for example, if a rental company has £10,000,000 Public Liability Insurance than the company should ensure that its contractors (including freelancers) also hold £10,000,000 Public Liability Insurance. This is normally a requirement of the "Bona fide Contractors" clause of your insurance policy; failure to ensure contractors (including Freelancers) have the required level of insurance (or even worse, no insurance) will almost certainly invalidate your insurance in the event of a claim.

The cost of Public/Employers Liability Insurance has increased substantially in the past few years and further rises are expected. There are several reasons for this including uncertainty and a lack of understanding of our industry by insurance underwriters: the September 11th disaster, an increase in the number of huge insurance claims, the number of individuals and organisations who do not meet minimum statutory health and safety regulations, the proliferation of no win – no fee legal schemes as advertised on TV and changes to health and safety legislation particularly in the area of asbestos disposal. Insurance companies have reacted by increasing premiums and by checking on health and safety competencies of clients.

There are numerous other types of insurance that are all relevant. For the self-employed working abroad then medical and repatriation insurance is essential in case of illness. The self-employed will also find unemployment and disability insurance a great comfort, and what would you do if you lost or had stolen your work tools and equipment? Are they insured?

- If you drive or use your car for work, are you insured for driving while at work or using your vehicle?
- If you give professional advice and information do you have Professional Indemnity Insurance?
- If you manufacture or supply products are you covered for those products?
- Some insurance is required by law – some by prudence.

With all the other expenses involved in setting up a business, it's tempting to have the minimum insurance required by law – insurance against risks to third parties. However, it makes sense to get adequate insurance to avoid the risk of losing it all.

Business insurance is usually divided into three fields:

- Liabilities
- Property and buildings
- Business assets and equipment (contents cover)

Employers' Liability

Once one employee is taken on it is required by law that the company takes out Employers Liability Insurance. The prescribed legal minimum is currently [2004] £10m of cover against bodily injury, illness or disease sustained in the course of employment. It is a legal requirement to display (in a prominent position so all employees can see it) a copy of the current Employers Liability Insurance certificate.

Public Liability

Definition: Legal liability to pay damages consequent upon bodily injury, illness or disease contracted by any other person, other than employees, or loss of or damage to their property caused by the insured. Limit of Indemnity is the maximum amount the insurance company will pay in the event of a claim being made. The limits are usually up to £5m but when working for another company, cover of £10m or more can be demanded.

Product Liability

Product Liability is your legal liability to pay damages consequent upon a defective product being used in the contract. Products liability insurance is a little more specialist. Businesses that supply products to other businesses or the public, from software to machine tools, are at risk if a faulty product causes damage or injury. Manufacturers of a product are usually at risk if things go wrong, but the liability can fall on a supplier if the maker of the product goes bust.

Professional Indemnity

Unfortunately, we live in litigious times. Businesses can be sued, rightly or wrongly, for vast damages over a range of complaints. Professional indemnity provides protection against any action by clients who believe they received bad or negligent services, and incurred a loss as a result. Most professional bodies have professional indemnity cover – in some cases it is compulsory. Anyone who supplies advice or services such as consultancy should consider professional indemnity.

Key Man Cover

Small firms depend heavily on a small number of key people. This cover cannot replace someone, but it can provide short-term financial help to reduce the impact.

Business Interruption

Even minor damage to your property could seriously disrupt your business leading to loss of income and extra expenses. Business interruption insurance will compensate for the short-fall in gross profit together with paying any increased working costs and extra accountants' fees incurred.

Goods in Transit

Goods in transit insurance covers goods against loss or damage while in your vehicle or when sent by carrier.

Property and Buildings

Buildings and contents can be insured against fire, lightning, explosion of gas and boilers used for domestic purposes without the addition of special perils such as explosion, riot, malicious damage, storm, flood, impact by aircraft, road and rail vehicles, escape of water from tanks or pipes and sprinkler leakage. 'All-risks' insurance gives wider cover including any accidental damage or loss not specifically excluded. However 'all-risks' will not cover wear and tear, electrical or mechanical breakdown and gradual deterioration which will be specifically stated in the policy document.

The business premises should be insured for their full rebuilding cost (including professional fees and the cost of site clearance) and not just for their market value. You may need expert advice to calculate the rebuilding cost, which often differs significantly from market value.

Business assets and equipment (contents cover)

Your stock should be insured for its cost price without profit. Plant and business equipment can be insured on either a 'replacement as new' or an 'indemnity' basis. If indemnity is chosen, wear and tear will be taken into account when settling any claims.

Engineering insurance provides cover against electrical or mechanical breakdown for most machinery, including computers. By law, many items of plant such as rigging and lifting machinery must be inspected regularly by a qualified person. Insurers can arrange to provide this service.

Contents are usually covered against theft providing there has been forcible and violent entry to or exit from the premises.

Damage to the building resulting from theft or attempted theft will also normally be covered. Theft by employees is usually not covered – cover against employee dishonesty can be arranged by a separate policy.

Money insurance is on an 'all-risks' basis and covers cash, cheques, postage stamps and certain other negotiable documents. Different limits will apply to money on the premises in and out of business hours, in safes, at the homes of directors or employees and in transit. There may be requirements in the policy relating to safe keys and the method of transit. Personal assault cover may be included, which will provide compensation for you or your employees following injury during theft or attempted theft of money.

    Robertson Taylor Insurance Brokers Ltd (+44 (0)207 510 1234)
    Precision Crew Cover (+44 (0)117 922 0420)
    Doodson Entertainment Insurance (+44 (0)207 444 6900)

    Please contact your insurance company or broker for up to date information relevant to your particular situation.

The Income Tax (Pay As You Earn) (Amendment No 2) Regulations 2015

These new regulations that come into force on April 6th 2015 seem to have slipped in below the radar for the events industry. As yet they are untried and untested but it basically means that if you send freelance crew out on a job for a client and you don't pay them under the PAYE scheme then you have to make regular reports to HMRC including the names and details of the crew you sent on the job and how much they were paid, etc. Much of the guidance refers to agencies and agency workers – but don't be fooled – it will equally apply to what we generally refer to as "freelancers" in our industry.

    I think we can see where this is going – another nail in the coffin of the self-employed as HMRC tightens up on getting more money out of us as the try to rid the world of what is known as false self-employment. This is where a person works on a self-employed basis when in fact they should be employed under PAYE and let's face it, our industry is full of such persons. So if you are a crewing company or security company and send out workers who are self-employed and not PAYE employees then you had best get the full information from HMRC or your tax advisor.

    An intermediary is any person who makes arrangements for an individual to work for a third party or be paid for work done for a third party. An employment intermediary is also commonly referred to as an agency but could also be a crewing or security company where self-employed /freelance crew are used.

    An intermediary is defined as any person who makes arrangements for an individual to work for a third party or be paid for work done for a third party. An employment intermediary is also commonly referred to as an agency.

From 6th April 2015, intermediaries must return details of all workers they place with clients where they do not operate PAYE on the workers' payments. The return will be a report (or reports) that must be sent to HMRC once every three months.

The new rules were introduced as a result of increasing abuse of the use of intermediary status, particularly through the use of false self-employment and supplying UK workers from an offshore location.

According to HMRC, 'both of these methods have been used to reduce employment taxes and avoid having to fulfil their legal employment rights and obligations'.

However, HMRC has confirmed that UK employers do not have to send HMRC reports if they:

- supply workers to provide their services to end clients and nobody else is involved; and
- operate PAYE when you pay those workers.

The rules take into account feedback to an HMRC consultation with intermediary representatives and wherever possible the final reporting requirements have been changed to reduce the regulatory burden, according to HMRC.

The legislation has been introduced under the Income Tax (Pay As You Earn) (Amendment No. 2) Regulations 2015 and will give HMRC information that will enable it to reduce false self-employment and abuse of offshore working.

Another area where HMRC are tightening up is in the definitions of who is in fact self-employed is if a contract or service exists and this time they are using time supervision, direction and control are as the basis. According to HMRC:

"A contract of service exists if these three conditions are fulfilled. (i) the servant agrees that, in consideration of a wage or other remuneration, he will provide his own work and skill in the performance of some service for his master (ii) **He agrees, expressly or impliedly that in the performance of that service he will be subject to the other's control in a sufficient degree to make that other master.** (iii) The *other provisions of the contract are consistent with its being a contract of service."*

When HMRC are considering if the provisions of the legislation apply to a person's job, they are looking at whether or not that person has the freedom to choose how they do their work, or instead, does someone have the power or authority over the worker to dictate how the work is done, by imposing control over them, subjecting them to supervision or giving them directions. HMRC consider supervision, direction and control are best defined as follows:

Supervision is someone overseeing a person doing work, to ensure that person is doing the work they are required to do and it is being done correctly to the required standard. Supervision can also involve helping the person where appropriate in order to develop their skills and knowledge.

Direction is someone making a person do is/her work in a certain way by providing them with instructions, guidance or advice as to how the work must be done. Someone providing direction will often coordinate the how the work is done, as it is being undertaken.

Control is someone dictating what work a person does and how they go about doing that work. Control also includes someone having the power to move the person from one job to another.

The main change in the law relates to the substitution of workers in a contract, which was backed as a sign of self-employment by the 2011 upper tier tribunal decision in HMRC v Talentcore.

Under the old rules, intermediaries were able to legally avoid paying 13.8% employers' tax, plus pensions and holiday pay, if workers could send a colleague to do their work for a client on their behalf.

This meant the workers were not providing a "personal service" and were therefore not subject to PAYE tax rules.

The revised rules close this loophole. So even if a worker can send colleagues to do their work they will still be classed as employed.

Health and Safety Consultants and Training Services to the Live Music and Events Industries

WE PROVIDE

- Health and Safety Consultancy
- Coordination of Licence Applications
- Event Safety Advisors
- Risk Assessments (including Fire Safety Risk Assessment by Qualified Fire Risk Assessors)
- Safety Documentation (Policies, Safe Systems of Work etc)
- Contractor Appraisal and Management
- PSA Safety Passport Training
- Fire Safety Training (Basic Fire Awareness and Fire Warden)
- Customised Training
- Contingency and Major Incident Planning
- SAG and ELT Liaison

For further details please visit our website

www.stagesafe.co.uk

info@stagesafe.co.uk

TEL: 07831 437062

For all your health and safety needs!

Health and Safety Management in the Live Music and Events Industry
by Chris Hannam

*Now available from Entertainment Technology Press Ltd
The Studio, High Green, Great Shelford, Cambridge, CB22 5EG UK
www.etbooks.co.uk*

First published in October 2004, Chris Hannam's major work on Health and Safety Management in the live music and events sector has been substantially revised. The title covers applications regarding all aspects of staging live entertainment events, and is an invaluable manual for managers and event organisers.

The book includes well thought-out and easy to understand sections on Risk Assessment and Safety Method Statements, Effective Health and Safety Policy, Selection of Personnel, Crowd Management, Communications, Performance Management, Environmental Safety to name but a few, as well as comprehensive chapters on all of the legal frameworks for Machinery, Fire Safety, Work Equipment, Employers Liability, Occupiers Liability, Accident Reporting and RIDDOR, PPE, Working at Height, LOLER, Special Effects, Temporary Structures, First Aid, Traffic Management, COSHH, Working Time Regulations and many more, this text covers all of the HSE and non-HSE publications in a well-managed and logical handbook.

Reviewing the second edition for Entertainment Technology magazine, John-Paul Greenock says: "Chris Hannam's book is an essential text for anyone who works within the Live Production Industry and should be the standard guide for promotion via our trade bodies. It dovetails effortlessly with the Event Safety Guide (Purple Guide) and sits effectively alongside the long awaited Safety Passport Scheme run under the Production Services Association. Chris, a leading provider of the scheme in the UK, initially introduced the idea of Safety Passports to the PSA, and subsequently developed the course as part of a safety passport working group. "I am pleased to have re-discovered, and thoroughly recommend Health and Safety Management in the Live Music and Events Industry, by one of the world's leading industry experts."

Health and Safety Management in the Live Music and Event Technical Production Industry Industry
A Guide for Employees and the self-Employed
by Chris Hannam

Now available from Entertainment Technology Press Ltd
The Studio, High Green, Great Shelford, Cambridge, CB22 5EG UK
www.etbooks.co.uk

A Review by Rose Durbin and Johnny Haskett

Chris Hannam has provided us with a comprehensive and accessible guide to health and safety in the live entertainment and technical event industries. This book is designed to accompany the various Safety Passport schemes and to help candidates gain a clear understanding of what is an issue of critical importance to an ever-changing profession.

As more and more young people are entering the industry from colleges and universities, it is imperative that publications such as this one are readily available to both students and seasoned professionals. It is high time that educational establishments and those in the private sector who run courses associated with the entertainment industries realize the importance of embedding best practice into their curriculum content.

This book will surely go a long way to encourage that, as it is pertinent to the various circumstances in which people entering the industry could find themselves. The author's expertise in the subject is clearly demonstrated in this publication and this guide will provide invaluable direction to anyone who engages with its content. As the introduction to this book sadly states, we seem to be lead to believe by the press etc. that "Health and Safety" is a set of outrageous rules designed to hinder our working life and get people out of lawsuits.

What this book clearly and concisely points out is that not only are these regulations common sense but are necessary to maintain a safe working environment. It is great that a book has finally been aimed at the music and events industry, and makes us aware that even in the smallest of working environments (small clubs and the like) that we are all obliged to think and act seriously with safety in mind.

As it is still an industry that doesn't seem to require any formal training at all levels, it is increasingly important that we all take our responsibilities seriously to maintain a risk free environment for ourselves and our colleagues to work in.

ENTERTAINMENT TECHNOLOGY PRESS

FREE SUBSCRIPTION SERVICE

Keeping Up To Date with

Health and Safety Management for Tour and Production Managers

and

Self-Employment in the Live Music and Events Industry

Entertainment Technology titles are continually up-dated, and all major changes and additions are listed in date order in the relevant dedicated area of the publisher's website. Simply go to the front page of www.etnow.com and click on the BOOKS button. From there you can locate the title and be connected through to the latest information and services related to the publication.

The author of the title welcomes comments and suggestions about the book and can be contacted by email at: info@stagesafe.co.uk

Titles Published by Entertainment Technology Press

50 Rigging Calls *Chris Higgs, Cristiano Giavedoni 246pp* **£16.95**
ISBN: 9781904031758
Chris Higgs, author of ETP's two leading titles on rigging, An Introduction to Rigging in the Entertainment Industry and Rigging for Entertainment: Regulations and Practice, has collected together 50 articles he has provided regularly for Lighting + Sound International magazine from 2005 to date. They provide a wealth of information for those practising the craft within the entertainment technology industry. The book is profusely illustrated with caricature drawings by Christiano Giavedoni, featuring the popular rigging expert Mario.

ABC of Theatre Jargon *Francis Reid 106pp* **£9.95** ISBN: 9781904031093
This glossary of theatrical terminology explains the common words and phrases that are used in normal conversation between actors, directors, designers, technicians and managers.

Aluminium Structures in the Entertainment Industry *Peter Hind 234pp* **£24.95**
ISBN: 9781904031062
Aluminium Structures in the Entertainment Industry aims to educate the reader in all aspects of the design and safe usage of temporary and permanent aluminium structures specific to the entertainment industry – such as roof structures, PA towers, temporary staging, etc.

AutoCAD – A Handbook for Theatre Users *David Ripley 340pp* **£29.95**
ISBN: 9781904031741
From 'Setting Up' to 'Drawing in Three Dimensions' via 'Drawings Within Drawings', this compact and fully illustrated guide to AutoCAD covers everything from the basics to full colour rendering and remote 3D plotting. Third, completely revised edition, June 2014.

Automation in the Entertainment Industry – A User's Guide *Mark Ager and John Hastie 382pp* **£29.95** ISBN: 9781904031581
In the last 15 years, there has been a massive growth in the use of automation in entertainment, especially in theatres, and it is now recognised as its own discipline. However, it is still only used in around 5% of theatres worldwide. In the next 25 years, given current growth patterns, that figure will rise to 30%. This will mean that the majority of theatre personnel, including directors, designers, technical staff, actors and theatre management, will come into contact with automation for the first time at some point in their careers. This book is intended to provide insights and practical advice from those who use automation, to help the first-time user understand the issues and avoid the pitfalls in its implementation.

Basics – A Beginner's Guide to Lighting Design *Peter Coleman 92pp* **£9.95**
ISBN: 9781904031413
The fourth in the author's 'Basics' series, this title covers the subject area in four main sections: The Concept, Practical Matters, Related Issues and The Design Into Practice. In an area that is difficult to be definitive, there are several things that cross all the boundaries of all lighting design and it's these areas that the author seeks to help with.

Basics – A Beginner's Guide to Special Effects *Peter Coleman 82pp* **£9.95**
ISBN: 9781904031338
This title introduces newcomers to the world of special effects. It describes all types of special effects including pyrotechnic, smoke and lighting effects, projections, noise machines, etc. It places emphasis on the safe storage, handling and use of pyrotechnics.

Basics – A Beginner's Guide to Stage Lighting *Peter Coleman 86pp* **£9.95**
ISBN: 9781904031208
This title does what it says: it introduces newcomers to the world of stage lighting. It will not teach the reader the art of lighting design, but will teach beginners much about the 'nuts and bolts' of stage lighting.

Basics – A Beginner's Guide to Stage Sound *Peter Coleman 86pp* **£9.95**
ISBN: 9781904031277
This title does what it says: it introduces newcomers to the world of stage sound. It will not teach the reader the art of sound design, but will teach beginners much about the background to sound reproduction in a theatrical environment.

Basics: A Beginner's Guide to Stage Management *Peter Coleman 64pp* **£7.95**
ISBN: 9781904031475
The fifth in Peter Coleman's popular 'Basics' series, this title provides a practical insight into, and the definition of, the role of stage management. Further chapters describe Cueing or 'Calling' the Show (the Prompt Book), and the Hardware and Training for Stage Management. This is a book about people and systems, without which most of the technical equipment used by others in the performance workplace couldn't function.

Building Better Theaters *Michael Mell 180pp* **£16.95** ISBN: 9781904031406
A title within our Consultancy Series, this book describes the process of designing a theatre, from the initial decision to build through to opening night. Michael Mell's book provides a step-by-step guide to the design and construction of performing arts facilities. Chapters discuss: assembling your team, selecting an architect, different construction methods, the architectural design process, construction of the theatre, theatrical systems and equipment, the stage, backstage, the auditorium, ADA requirements and the lobby. Each chapter clearly describes what to expect and how to avoid surprises. It is a must-read for architects, planners, performing arts groups, educators and anyone who may be considering building or renovating a theatre.

Carry on Fading *Francis Reid 216pp* **£20.00** ISBN: 9781904031642
This is a record of five of the best years of the author's life. Years so good that the only downside is the pangs of guilt at enjoying such contentment in a world full of misery induced by greed, envy and imposed ideologies. Fortunately Francis' DNA is high on luck, optimism and blessing counting.

Case Studies in Crowd Management
Chris Kemp, Iain Hill, Mick Upton, Mark Hamilton 206pp **£16.95**
ISBN: 9781904031482
This important work has been compiled from a series of research projects carried out by the staff of the Centre for Crowd Management and Security Studies at Buckinghamshire Chilterns University College (now Bucks New University), and seminar work carried out in Berlin and Groningen with partner Yourope. It includes case studies, reports and a crowd management safety plan for a major outdoor rock concert, safe management of rock concerts utilising a triple barrier safety system and pan-European Health & Safety Issues.

Case Studies in Crowd Management, Security and Business Continuity
Chris Kemp, Patrick Smith 274pp **£24.95** ISBN: 9781904031635
The creation of good case studies to support work in progress and to give answers to those seeking guidance in their quest to come to terms with perennial questions is no easy task. The first Case Studies in Crowd Management book focused mainly on a series of festivals and events that had a number of issues which required solving. This book focuses on a series of events that had major issues that impacted on the every day delivery of the events researched.

Close Protection – The Softer Skills *Geoffrey Padgham 132pp* **£11.95**
ISBN: 9781904031390
This is the first educational book in a new 'Security Series' for Entertainment Technology Press, and it coincides with the launch of the new 'Protective Security Management' Foundation Degree at Buckinghamshire Chilterns University College (now Bucks New University). The author is a former full-career Metropolitan Police Inspector from New Scotland Yard with 27 years' experience of close protection (CP). For 22 of those years he specialised in operations and senior management duties with the Royalty Protection Department at Buckingham Palace, followed by five years in the private security industry specialising in CP training design and delivery. His wealth of protection experience comes across throughout the text, which incorporates sound advice and exceptional practical guidance, subtly separating fact from fiction. This publication is an excellent form of reference material for experienced operatives, students and trainees.

A Comparative Study of Crowd Behaviour at Two Major Music Events
Chris Kemp, Iain Hill, Mick Upton 78pp **£7.95** ISBN: 9781904031253
A compilation of the findings of reports made at two major live music concerts, and in particular crowd behaviour, which is followed from ingress to egress.

Control Freak *Wayne Howell 270pp* **£28.95** ISBN: 9781904031550
Control Freak is the second book by Wayne Howell. It provides an in depth study of DMX512 and the new RDM (Remote Device Management) standards. The book is aimed at both users and developers and provides a wealth of real world information based on the author's twenty year experience of lighting control.

Copenhagen Opera House *Richard Brett and John Offord 272pp* **£32.00**
ISBN: 9781904031420
Completed in a little over three years, the Copenhagen Opera House opened with a royal gala performance on 15th January 2005. Built on a spacious brown-field site, the building is a landmark venue and this book provides the complete technical background story to an opera house set to become a benchmark for future design and planning. Sixteen chapters by relevant experts involved with the project cover everything from the planning of the auditorium and studio stage, the stage engineering, stage lighting and control and architectural lighting through to acoustic design and sound technology plus technical summaries.

Corporate Event Production – Effective, face-to-face, corporate communication or Reaching 'The guy at the back, with bad eyesight - who'd rather be in the bar'
David Clement 324pp **£29.95** ISBN: 9781904031840
A real-world insight into a specific industry sector: Corporate Event Production – the business of face-to-face communication. What it actually feels like to work in live events. The subtitle of 'Reaching the guy at the back with bad eyesight – who'd rather be in the bar' encapsulates the producer's challenge of creating an equally memorable experience for all attendees.
Structured around the project timeline – from receipt of a brief, to creative response and pitching, through pre-production design and planning to creating and directing the show on the day – the book is full of industry anecdotes, over 160 reference images, useful tips and guidelines. The stage-by-stage process of designing an engaging and truly effective live event.

Cue 80 *Francis Reid 310pp* **£17.95** ISBN: 9781904031659
Although Francis Reid's work in theatre has been visual rather than verbal, writing has provided crucial support. Putting words on paper has been the way in which he organised and clarified his thoughts. And in his self-confessed absence of drawing skills, writing has helped him find words to communicate his visual thinking in discussions with the rest of the creative team. As a by-product, this process of searching for the right words to help formulate and analyse ideas has resulted in half-a-century of articles in theatre journals. Cue 80 is an anthology of these articles and is released in celebration of Francis' 80th birthday.

The DMX 512-A Handbook – Design and Implementation of DMX Enabled Products and Networks *James Eade 150pp* **£13.95** ISBN: 9781904031727
This guidebook was originally conceived as a guide to the new DMX512-A standard on behalf of the ESTA Controls Protocols Working Group (CPWG). It has subsequently been updated and is aimed at all levels of reader from technicians working with or servicing equipment in the field as well as manufacturers looking to build in DMX control to their lighting products. It also gives thorough guidance to consultants and designers looking to design DMX networks.

Electric Shadows: an Introduction to Video and Projection on Stage *Nick Moran 234pp* **£23.95**   ISBN: 9781904031734
Electric Shadows aims to guide the emerging video designer through the many simple and difficult technical and aesthetic choices and decisions he or she has to make in taking their design from outline idea through to realisation. The main body of the book takes the reader through the process of deciding what content will be projected onto what screen or screens to make the best overall production design. The book will help you make electric shadows that capture the attention of your audience, to help you tell your stories in just the way you want.

Electrical Safety for Live Events   *Marco van Beek 98pp*   **£16.95**   ISBN: 9781904031284
This title covers electrical safety regulations and good practise pertinent to the entertainment industries and includes some basic electrical theory as well as clarifying the "do's and don't's" of working with electricity.

Entertainment Electronics   *Anton Woodward 154pp*   **£15.95**   ISBN: 9781904031819
Electronic engineering in theatres has become quite prevalent in recent years, whether for lighting, sound, automation or props – so it has become an increasingly important skill for the theatre technician to possess. This book is intended to give the theatre technician a good grasp of the fundamental principles of electronics without getting too bogged down with maths so that many of the mysteries of electronics are revealed.

Entertainment in Production Volume 1: 1994-1999   *Rob Halliday 254pp*   **£24.95** ISBN: 9781904031512
Entertainment in Production Volume 2: 2000-2006   *Rob Halliday 242poo*   £24.95 ISBN: 9781904031529
Rob Halliday has a dual career as a lighting designer/programmer and author and in these two volumes he provides the intriguing but comprehensive technical background stories behind the major musical productions and other notable projects spanning the period 1994 to 2005. Having been closely involved with the majority of the events described, the author is able to present a first-hand and all-encompassing portrayal of how many of the major shows across the past decade came into being. From *Oliver!* and *Miss Saigon* to *Mamma Mia!* and *Mary Poppins*, here the complete technical story unfolds. The books, which are profusely illustrated, are in large part an adapted selection of articles that first appeared in the magazine *Lighting&Sound International*.

Entertainment Technology Yearbook 2008   *John Offord 220pp*   **£14.95** ISBN: 9781904031543
The Entertainment Technology Yearbook 2008 covers the year 2007 and includes picture coverage of major industry exhibitions in Europe compiled from the pages of Entertainment Technology magazine and the etnow.com website, plus articles and pictures of production, equipment and project highlights of the year.

The Exeter Theatre Fire   *David Anderson 202pp*   **£24.95**   ISBN: 9781904031130
This title is a fascinating insight into the events that led up to the disaster at the Theatre Royal, Exeter, on the night of September 5th 1887. The book details what went wrong, and the lessons that were learned from the event.

Fading into Retirement *Francis Reid 124pp* **£17.95**   ISBN: 9781904031352
This is the final book in Francis Reid's fading trilogy which, with Fading Light and Carry on Fading, updates the Hearing the Light record of places visited, performances seen, and people met. Never say never, but the author uses the 'final' label because decreasing mobility means that his ability to travel is diminished to the point that his life is now contained within a very few square miles. His memories are triggered by over 600 CDs, half of them Handel and 100 or so DVDs supplemented by a rental subscription to LOVEFiLM.

Fading Light – A Year in Retirement *Francis Reid 136pp* **£14.95** ISBN: 9781904031352
Francis Reid, the lighting industry's favourite author, describes a full year in retirement. "Old age is much more fun than I expected," he says. Fading Light describes visits and experiences to the author's favourite theatres and opera houses, places of relaxation and re-visits to scholarly institutions.

Focus on Lighting Technology *Richard Cadena 120pp* **£17.95**   ISBN: 9781904031147
This concise work unravels the mechanics behind modern performance lighting and appeals to designers and technicians alike. Packed with clear, easy-to-read diagrams, the book provides excellent explanations behind the technology of performance lighting.

The Followspot Guide *Nick Mobsby 450pp*   **£28.95**   ISBN: 9781904031499
The first in ETP's Equipment Series, Nick Mobsby's Followspot Guide tells you everything you need to know about followspots, from their history through to maintenance and usage. Its pages include a technical specification of 193 followspots from historical to the latest versions from major manufacturers.

From Ancient Rome to Rock 'n' Roll – a Review of the UK Leisure Security Industry *Mick Upton 198pp*   **£14.95**   ISBN: 9781904031505
From stewarding, close protection and crowd management through to his engagement as a senior consultant Mick Upton has been ever present in the events industry. A founder of ShowSec International in 1982 he was its chairman until 2000. The author has led the way on training within the sector. He set up the ShowSec Training Centre and has acted as a consultant at the Bramshill Police College. He has been prominent in the development of courses at Buckinghamshire New University where he was awarded a Doctorate in 2005. Mick has received numerous industry awards. His book is a personal account of the development and professionalism of the sector across the past 50 years.

Gobos for Image Projection *Michael Hall and Julie Harper 176pp* **£25.95** ISBN: 9781904031628
In this first published book dedicated totally to the gobo, the authors take the reader through from the history of projection to the development of the present day gobo. And there is broad practical advice and ample reference information to back it up. A feature of the work is the inclusion, interspersed throughout the text, of comment and personal experience in the use and application of gobos from over 25 leading lighting designers worldwide.

Health and Safety Aspects in the Live Music Industry *Chris Kemp, Iain Hill 300pp*
£30.00 ISBN: 9781904031222
This major work includes chapters on various safety aspects of live event production and is written by specialists in their particular areas of expertise.

Health and Safety in the Live Music and Event Technical Produciton Industry
Chris Hannam 74pp **£12.95** ISBN: 9781904031802
This book covers the real basics of health and safety in the live music and event production industry in a simple jargon free manner that can also be used as the perfect student course note accompaniment to the various safety passport schemes that now exist in our industry.

Health and Safety Management for Tour and Production Managers and
Self-Employment in the Live Music and Events Industry
Chris Hannam 136pp **£11.95** ISBN: 9781904031864
Two books in one: **Health and Safety Management for Tour and Production Managers** is designed to give simple, basic health and safety information to bands, artists, tour, stage and production managers, crew chiefs, heads of department, supervisors or line managers and has been designed as a follow on from *Health And Safety in the Live Music and Event Technical Production Industry*. It will also be of use to local crew companies, especially their crew chiefs and managers.
The second book is **Self-Employment in the Live Music and Events Industry**
A Guide for the Self-Employed and those who use the services of the Self-Employed

Health and Safety Management in the Live Music and Events Industry *Chris Hannam 480pp* **£25.95** ISBN: 9781904031307
This title covers the health and safety regulations and their application regarding all aspects of staging live entertainment events, and is an invaluable manual for production managers and event organisers.

Hearing the Light – 50 Years Backstage *Francis Reid 280pp* **£24.95**
ISBN: 9781904031185
This highly enjoyable memoir delves deeply into the theatricality of the industry. The author's almost fanatical interest in opera, his formative period as lighting designer at Glyndebourne and his experiences as a theatre administrator, writer and teacher make for a broad and unique background.

Introduction to Live Sound *Roland Higham 174pp* **£16.95**
ISBN: 9781904031796
This new title aims to provide working engineers and newcomers alike with a concise knowledge base that explains some of the theory and principles that they will encounter every day. It should provide for the student and newcomer to the field a valuable compendium of helpful knowledge.

An Introduction to Rigging in the Entertainment Industry *Chris Higgs 272pp* **£24.95**
ISBN: 9781904031123
This title is a practical guide to rigging techniques and practices and also thoroughly covers safety issues and discusses the implications of working within recommended guidelines and regulations. Second edition revised September 2008.

Let There be Light – Entertainment Lighting Software Pioneers in Conversation
Robert Bell 390pp **£32.00**   ISBN: 9781904031246
Robert Bell interviews a distinguished group of software engineers working on entertainment lighting ideas and products.

Light and Colour Filters *Michael Hall and Eddie Ruffell 286pp* **£23.95**
ISBN: 9781904031598
Written by two acknowledged and respected experts in the field, this book is destined to become the standard reference work on the subject. The title chronicles the development and use of colour filters and also describes how colour is perceived and how filters function. Up-to-date reference tables will help the practitioner make better and more specific choices of colour.

Lighting for Roméo and Juliette *John Offord 172pp* **£26.95** ISBN: 9781904031161
John Offord describes the making of the Vienna State Opera production from the lighting designer's viewpoint – from the point where director Jürgen Flimm made his decision not to use scenery or sets and simply employ the expertise of lighting designer Patrick Woodroffe.

Lighting Systems for TV Studios *Nick Mobsby 570pp* **£45.00** ISBN: 9781904031000
Lighting Systems for TV Studios, now in its second edition, is the first book specifically written on the subject and has become the 'standard' resource work for studio planning and design covering the key elements of system design, luminaires, dimming, control, data networks and suspension systems as well as detailing the infrastructure items such as cyclorama, electrical and ventilation. TV lighting principles are explained and some history on TV broadcasting, camera technology and the equipment is provided to help set the scene! The second edition includes applications for sine wave and distributed dimming, moving lights, Ethernet and new cool lamp technology.

Lighting Techniques for Theatre-in-the-Round *Jackie Staines 188pp* **£24.95**
ISBN: 9781904031017
Lighting Techniques for Theatre-in-the-Round is a unique reference source for those working on lighting design for theatre-in-the-round for the first time. It is the first title to be published specifically on the subject and it also provides some anecdotes and ideas for more challenging shows, and attempts to blow away some of the myths surrounding lighting in this format.

Lighting the Diamond Jubilee Concert *Durham Marenghi 102pp* **£19.95**
ISBN: 9781904031673
In this highly personal landmark document the show's lighting designer Durham Marenghi pays tribute to the team of industry experts who each played an important role in bringing

the Diamond Jubilee Concert to fruition, both for television and live audiences. The book contains colour production photography throughout and describes the production processes and the thinking behind them. In his Foreword, BBC Executive Producer Guy Freeman states: "Working with the whole lighting team on such a special project was a real treat for me and a fantastic achievement for them, which the pages of this book give a remarkable insight into."

Lighting the Stage *Francis Reid 120pp* **£14.95** ISBN: 9781904031086
Lighting the Stage discusses the human relationships involved in lighting design – both between people, and between these people and technology. The book is written from a highly personal viewpoint and its 'thinking aloud' approach is one that Francis Reid has used in his writings over the past 30 years.

Miscellany of Lighting and Stagecraft *Michael Hall & Julie Harper 222pp* **£22.95**
ISBN: 9781904031680
This title will help schools, colleges, amateurs, technicians and all those interested in practical theatre and performance to understand, in an entertaining and informative way, the key backstage skills. Within its pages, numerous professionals share their own special knowledge and expertise, interspersed with diversions of historic interest and anecdotes from those practising at the front line of the industry. As a result, much of the advice and skills set out have not previously been set in print. The editors' intention with this book is to provide a Miscellany that is not ordered or categorised in strict fashion, but rather encourages the reader to flick through or dip into it, finding nuggets of information and anecdotes to entertain, inspire and engender curiosity – also to invite further research or exploration and generally encourage people to enter the industry and find out for themselves.

Mr Phipps' Theatre *Mark Jones, John Pick 172pp* £17.95 ISBN: 9781904031383
Mark Jones and John Pick describe "The Sensational Story of Eastbourne's Royal Hippodrome" – formerly Eastbourne Theatre Royal. An intriguing narrative, the book sets the story against a unique social history of the town. Peter Longman, former director of The Theatres Trust, provides the Foreword.

Northen Lights *Michael Northen 256pp* **£17.95** ISBN: 9781904031666
Many books have been written by famous personalities in the theatre about their lives and work. However this is probably one of the first memoirs by someone who has spent his entire career behind scenes, and not in front of the footlights. As a lighting designer and as consultant to designers and directors, Michael Northen worked through an exciting period of fifty years of theatrical history from the late nineteen thirties in theatres in the UK and abroad, and on productions ranging from Shakespeare, opera and ballet to straight plays, pantomimes and cabaret. This is not a complicated technical text book, but is intended to give an insight into some of the 300 productions in which he had been involved and some of the directors, the designers and backstage staff he have worked with, viewed from a new angle.

Pages From Stages *Anthony Field 204pp* **£17.95** ISBN: 9781904031260
Anthony Field explores the changing style of theatres including interior design, exterior design, ticket and seat prices, and levels of service, while questioning whether the theatre still exists as a place of entertainment for regular theatre-goers.

People, Places, Performances *Remembered by Francis Reid 60pp* **£8.95** ISBN: 9781904031765
In growing older, the Author has found that memories, rather than featuring the events, increasingly tend to focus on the people who caused them, the places where they happened and the performances that arose. So Francis Reid has used these categories in endeavouring to compile a brief history of the second half of the twentieth century.

Performing Arts Technical Training Handbook 2013/2014 *ed: John Offord 304pp* **£19.95** ISBN: 9781904031710
Published in association with the ABTT (Association of British Theatre Technicians), this important Handbook, now in its third edition, includes fully detailed and indexed entries describing courses on backstage crafts offered by over 100 universities and colleges across the UK. A completely new research project, with accompanying website, the title also includes articles with advice for those considering a career 'behind the scenes', together with contact information and descriptions of the major organisations involved with industry training – plus details of companies offering training within their own premises.

Practical Dimming *Nick Mobsby 364pp* **£22.95** ISBN: 97819040313444
This important and easy to read title covers the history of electrical and electronic dimming, how dimmers work, current dimmer types from around the world, planning of a dimming system, looking at new sine wave dimming technology and distributed dimming. Integration of dimming into different performance venues as well as the necessary supporting electrical systems are fully detailed. Significant levels of information are provided on the many different forms and costs of potential solutions as well as how to plan specific solutions. Architectural dimming for the likes of hotels, museums and shopping centres is included. Practical Dimming is a companion book to Practical DMX and is designed for all involved in the use, operation and design of dimming systems.

Practical DMX *Nick Mobsby 276pp* **£16.95** ISBN: 9781904031369
In this highly topical and important title the author details the principles of DMX, how to plan a network, how to choose equipment and cables, with data on products from around the world, and how to install DMX networks for shows and on a permanently installed basis. The easy style of the book and the helpful fault finding tips, together with a review of different DMX testing devices provide an ideal companion for all lighting technicians and system designers. An introduction to Ethernet and Canbus networks are provided as well as tips on analogue networks and protocol conversion. It also includes a chapter on Remote Device Management.

A Practical Guide to Health and Safety in the Entertainment Industry
Marco van Beek 120pp **£14.95**   ISBN: 9781904031048
This book is designed to provide a practical approach to Health and Safety within the Live Entertainment and Event industry. It gives industry-pertinent examples, and seeks to break down the myths surrounding Health and Safety.

Production Management *Joe Aveline 134pp* **£17.95**   ISBN: 9781904031109
Joe Aveline's book is an in-depth guide to the role of the Production Manager, and includes real-life practical examples and 'Aveline's Fables' – anecdotes of his experiences with real messages behind them.

Rigging for Entertainment: Regulations and Practice *Chris Higgs 156pp*   **£19.95**
ISBN: 9781904031215
Continuing where he left off with his highly successful An Introduction to Rigging in the Entertainment Industry, Chris Higgs' second title covers the regulations and use of equipment in greater detail.

Rock Solid Ethernet *Wayne Howell 304pp*   **£23.95**   ISBN: 9781904031697
Now in its third completely revised and reset edition, Rock Solid Ethernet is aimed specifically at specifiers, installers and users of entertainment industry systems, and will give the reader a thorough grounding in all aspects of computer networks, whatever industry they may work in. The inclusion of historical and technical 'sidebars' make for an enjoyable as well as an informative read.

Sixty Years of Light Work *Fred Bentham 450pp*   **£26.95**   ISBN: 9781904031079
This title is an autobiography of one of the great names behind the development of modern stage lighting equipment and techniques. It includes a complete facsimile of the famous Strand Electric Catalogue of May 1936 – a reference work in itself.

Sound for the Stage *Patrick Finelli 218pp*   **£24.95**   ISBN: 9781904031154
Patrick Finelli's thorough manual covering all aspects of live and recorded sound for performance is a complete training course for anyone interested in working in the field of stage sound, and is a must for any student of sound.

Stage Automation *Anton Woodward 128pp*   **£12.95**   ISBN: 9781904031567
The purpose of this book is to explain the stage automation techniques used in modern theatre to achieve some of the spectacular visual effects seen in recent years. The book is targeted at automation operators, production managers, theatre technicians, stage engineering machinery manufacturers and theatre engineering students. Topics are covered in sufficient detail to provide an insight into the thought processes that the stage automation engineer has to consider when designing a control system to control stage machinery in a modern theatre. The author has worked on many stage automation projects and developed the award-winning Impressario stage automation system.

Stage Lighting Design in Britain: The Emergence of the Lighting Designer, 1881-1950
Nigel Morgan 300pp **£17.95** ISBN: 9781904031345
This title sets out to ascertain the main course of events and the controlling factors that determined the emergence of the theatre lighting designer in Britain, starting with the introduction of incandescent electric light to the stage, and ending at the time of the first public lighting design credits around 1950. The book explores the practitioners, equipment, installations and techniques of lighting design.

Stage Lighting for Theatre Designers *Nigel Morgan 124pp* **£17.95**
ISBN: 9781904031192
This is an updated second edition of Nigel Morgan's popular book for students of theatre design – outlining all the techniques of stage lighting design.

Technical Marketing – Ideas for Engineers *David Brooks. 376pp* **£26.95**
ISBN: 9781904031857
When *Technical Marketing Techniques* was published in 2000, marketing was poised on the threshold of a new era. What advertising and design agencies then termed 'new media' was merely a glimpse of what was to follow as the Internet came to dominate and transform the way we did things. We coined the term Technical Marketing to describe a new way of operating for businesses and how they marketed their products and services on a global platform. 'Technical Marketing – Ideas for Engineers' retains a major opening section covering traditional marketing theory and then in the second section demonstrates how online and offline techniques can be integrated into an effective marketing communications plan. The final section of the book reviews the still evolving possibilities of digital marketing which is beginning to re write the rules of marketing.

Technical Standards for Places of Entertainment (2015) *ABTT 366pp A4* **£60.00**
ISBN: 9781904031833
Technical Standards for Places of Entertainment details the necessary physical standards required for entertainment venues. Known in the industry as the "Yellow Book" the latest completely revised edition was first published in June 2015.

Theatre Engineering and Stage Machinery *Toshiro Ogawa 332pp* **£30.00**
ISBN: 9781904031024
Theatre Engineering and Stage Machinery is a unique reference work covering every aspect of theatrical machinery and stage technology in global terms, and across the complete historical spectrum. Revised February 2007.

Theatre Lighting in the Age of Gas *Terence Rees 232pp* **£24.95**
ISBN: 9781904031178
Entertainment Technology Press has republished this valuable historic work previously produced by the Society for Theatre Research in 1978. Theatre Lighting in the Age of Gas investigates the technological and artistic achievements of theatre lighting engineers from the 1700s to the late Victorian period.

Theatre Space: A Rediscovery Reported *Francis Reid 238pp* **£19.95**
ISBN: 9781904031437
In the post-war world of the 1950s and 60s, the format of theatre space became a matter for a debate that aroused passions of an intensity unknown before or since. The proscenium arch was clearly identified as the enemy, accused of forming a barrier to disrupt the relations between the actor and audience. An uneasy fellow-traveller at the time, Francis Reid later recorded his impressions whilst enjoying performances or working in theatres old and new and this book is an important collection of his writings in various theatrical journals from 1969-2001 including his contribution to the Cambridge Guide to the Theatre in 1988. It reports some of the flavour of the period when theatre architecture was rediscovering its past in a search to establish its future.

The Theatres and Concert Halls of Fellner and Helmer *Michael Sell 246pp* **£23.95**
ISBN: 9781904031772
This is the first British study of the works of the prolific Fellner and Helmer Atelier which was active from 1871-1914 during which time they produced over 80 theatre designs and are second in quantity only to Frank Matcham, to whom reference is made.
This period is one of great change as a number of serious theatre fires which included Nice and Vienna had the effect of the introduction of safety legislation which affected theatre design. This study seeks to show how Fellner and Helmer and Frank Matcham dealt with this increasing safety legislation, in particular the way in which safety was built into their new three part theatres equipped with iron stages, safety curtains, electricity and appropriate access and egress and, in the Vienna practice, how this was achieved across 13 countries.

Theatres of Achievement *John Higgins 302pp* **£29.95** ISBN: 9781904031376
John Higgins affectionately describes the history of 40 distinguished UK theatres in a personal tribute, each uniquely illustrated by the author. Completing each profile is colour photography by Adrian Eggleston.

A Theatric Miscellany *Francis Reid 154pp* **£15.95** ISBN: 9781904031871
This book is about memories. Some of them are highlights of the author's life. Recall of other, more routine events, is triggered by discovery of a cache of sundry articles. A few make predictions that are still relevant but most guess the future wrongly. Either way, they make a small contribution to history.

Theatric Tourist *Francis Reid 220pp* **£19.95** ISBN: 9781904031468
Theatric Tourist is the delightful story of Francis Reid's visits across more than 50 years to theatres, theatre museums, performances and even movie theme parks. In his inimitable style, the author involves the reader within a personal experience of venues from the Legacy of Rome to theatres of the Renaissance and Eighteenth Century Baroque and the Gustavian Theatres of Stockholm. His performance experiences include Wagner in Beyreuth, the Pleasures of Tivoli and Wayang in Singapore. This is a 'must have' title for those who are as "incurably stagestruck" as the author.

Through the Viewfinder *Jeremy Hoare 276pp* **£21.95** ISBN:: 9781904031574
Do you want to be a top television cameraman? Well this is going to help!
Through the Viewfinder is aimed at media students wanting to be top professional television cameramen – but it will also be of interest to anyone who wants to know what goes on behind the cameras that bring so much into our homes.
The author takes his own opinionated look at how to operate a television camera based on 23 years' experience looking through many viewfinders for a major ITV network company. Based on interviews with people he has worked with, all leaders in the profession, the book is based on their views and opinions and is a highly revealing portrait of what happens behind the scenes in television production from a cameraman's point of view.

Vectorworks for Theatre *Steve Macluskie 232pp* **£23.95** ISBN: 9781904031826
An essential reference manual for anyone using Vectorworks in the Theatre Industry. This book covers everything from introducing the basic tools to creating 3D design concepts and using worksheets to calculate stock usage and lighting design paperwork. A highly visual style using hundreds of high resolution screen images makes this a very easy book to follow whether novice or experienced user.

Walt Disney Concert Hall – The Backstage Story *Patricia MacKay & Richard Pilbrow 250pp* **£28.95** ISBN: 9781904031239
Spanning the 16-year history of the design and construction of the Walt Disney Concert Hall, this book provides a fresh and detailed behind the scenes story of the design and technology from a variety of viewpoints. This is the first book to reveal the "process" of the design of a concert hall.

Yesterday's Lights – A Revolution Reported *Francis Reid 352pp* **£26.95** ISBN: 9781904031321
Set to help new generations to be aware of where the art and science of theatre lighting is coming from – and stimulate a nostalgia trip for those who lived through the period, Francis Reid's latest book has over 350 pages dedicated to the task, covering the 'revolution' from the fifties through to the present day. Although this is a highly personal account of the development of lighting design and technology and he admits that there are 'gaps', you'd be hard put to find anything of significance missing.

Go to www.etbooks.co.uk for full details of above titles and secure online ordering facilities. Most books also available for Kindle.